TABLE OF CONTENTS

Foreword i
Preface v

Chapter 1: Who Needs a New Sales Methodology? 1
    Time for Some Myth-Busting 2
    But I Don't Need Another Methodology! 3
    Transactional to Consultative 4
    Today's Buyer 6
    A New Approach 7
    Can't I Get an App for That? 7
    Use Digital Tools for Support 9
    Time to Get REAL 11
    A History Lesson 12
    What Makes Buyers Tick 14
    The Modern Era of Sales 15
    The Postmodern Era of Sales 16

Chapter 2: Why REAL Selling Matters 19
    REAL Selling for the Long-term 20

Research Builds Competitive Differentiation......20
Engage Your Customer Like It's 1899......21
Become The Trusted Advisor......23
Lead to the Solution like Crown Royal......24
Why REAL Selling Matters......26

Chapter 3: R Is for Research......27
Know Your Customer......28
Know the Industry......29
Intent Is Your Superpower......31
Putting Customers in Perspective......34
R Is for Research: Thought Generator......37

Chapter 4: E Is for Engage......38
You Need a PAO!......39
You Need a LOU......42
Trust......43
Handling Objections......45
Customer-centricity......48
E Is for Engage: Thought Generator......49

Chapter 5: A Is for Advocate......50
Dwight Shrut Knows His Customer......52
Make It Easy to Buy from You......54
The Success Plan......56
Metrics to Measure Success......58
A Is for Advocate: Thought Generator......61

Chapter 6: L is for Lead to the Solution......62
The Best Idea Is When You Think of My Idea......63
Challenger Taught Us to Dance......64

REAL Selling

Carol L. Cohen

outskirts
press

REAL Selling
All Rights Reserved.
Copyright © 2022 Carol L. Cohen
v2.0

The opinions expressed in this manuscript are solely the opinions of the author and do not represent the opinions or thoughts of the publisher. The author has represented and warranted full ownership and/or legal right to publish all the materials in this book.

This book may not be reproduced, transmitted, or stored in whole or in part by any means, including graphic, electronic, or mechanical without the express written consent of the publisher except in the case of brief quotations embodied in critical articles and reviews.

Outskirts Press, Inc.
http://www.outskirtspress.com

ISBN: 978-1-9772-5198-5

Cover Photo © 2022 www.gettyimages.com. All rights reserved - used with permission.

Outskirts Press and the "OP" logo are trademarks belonging to Outskirts Press, Inc.

PRINTED IN THE UNITED STATES OF AMERICA

    The Expansion Sale 67
    The Roadmap To A Valued Partnership 68
    L Is for Lead to the Solution: Thought Generator 69

Chapter 7: Your Next Steps 70
    Hints and Tips 70
    REAL Reminders 72
    Don't Stop Learning 76
    In Closing 79

Acknowledgements 81

Foreword

By Becky Tise

When I was old enough to know a thing or two, my business partner and I decided to take a big risk and approach a small European company that we admired and ask if they'd ever considered starting up a U.S. operation. It turned out that they had considered it but hadn't ever found the people with the right backgrounds. With our previous experience we were a perfect fit, and so we found ourselves with the whole of the country, a blank slate, and wonderful consulting offerings to sell that nobody knew about. We had our work cut out for us.

We began to research who our target audience was and identified them by role. We went to work beating the heck out of LinkedIn and other resources to generate interest. Our objective was to get an audience with prospective buyers in a friendly, engaging environment where we could learn more about them. We decided that workshops were the perfect vehicle for us to present, question, listen, and learn. We already knew we had something that could help people; the idea behind the workshops was to provide them the education to lead our prospects to that same conclusion. We also knew that we had to provide some kind of value in the workshop just to get people to attend, whether they ended up buying from us or not.

We were able to engage people by tailoring communications to the things they were interested in and presenting the workshops as an opportunity to learn more about our consulting offerings that could help them achieve their objectives. Attendees also got the rare opportunity to network with their peers in other companies and industries. We also fed people, which is always a plus. Our mission was to find prospects with needs around team dynamics. Our workshops were designed to be engaging and interactive, using peer-to-peer coaching to get them thinking about their own teams, and ultimately, about how they might work with us.

Our mass "sheep dip" sessions worked much like a sales funnel. We were able to follow up with selected participants, obtaining further discovery meetings which were more like warm calls than cold calls since we'd already spent time together. With further customized research, we were able to turn leads from each workshop into closed business, and much to the amazement of our parent company, we were profitable in our first year.

It was an enormously satisfying feeling to be sitting across the table from someone we hadn't even known just a couple of months before and to be working on the timing and pricing of our consulting. Time after time, we were able to discover companies that needed our services and turn our venture from nonexistent to a multimillion-dollar operation in the first year.

We could say we were lucky, and we had our share, but we were very deliberate in how we invested our time to get to the end result. If you want to know how to do it, you are holding the answer in your hands. *REAL Selling* will give you a fresh approach to sales that really works, whether you are new to sales or wanting to up your game. Now, let's get REAL.

Becky Tise is the principal of 450 Market Group based on the seacoast of New Hampshire. She is happily married to her business partner and is a part-time consultant, musician, e-bike enthusiast, and type-1 diabetes warrior.

Preface

Several decades ago, the approach to teaching teachers was student-centered. At the time, it was a radical approach to education, and it set the new graduates apart from the "old-school" ways of lecture and test. While this was vastly different from the way education had been delivered previously, it gained rapid popularity. It is likely you have been participating in student-centered, project-based discovery sessions during your own education. I am a fourth-generation teacher, and it is the way that I studied and learned to be a certified high school teacher. This approach requires students to learn through discovery with the instructor acting as a guide on the side rather than a sage on the stage. Why am I talking about this? To understand the evolution of this most recent sales methodology, I felt a short trip along my own journey to it might put things in perspective.

Somewhere along my teaching career, I found myself in need of supplementing my income. I needed to get a second job, so I looked in the want ads and there it was: "Teachers! If you need a second job, this is the one for you." So, I headed into a retail sales situation with no idea if I would be successful. I ended up working in a commission-based camera store with nine locations throughout our state. We also offered the only one-hour photo development at that time and that brought in a lot of customers. I was the number-one seller every week. This surprised me on a weekly basis as I was a teacher, not a salesperson. I kept asking myself what I was doing that the salespeople were not. I began to believe that the student-centered approach to teaching was directly applicable to a customer-centric approach to selling.

I have vivid memories of the manager and his compatriot lead seller standing in the doorway greeting people as they came in. And if they saw someone in a nice suit looking like they had money to spend, they would buttonhole them in conversation, but anyone else they passed through to me. And I would usually sell them a large, expensive camera outfit. This happened repeatedly. They judged the customer by a single criterion, and I was listening to the customer instead. Picture this customer. In walks a guy in his twenties in jeans and tee shirt. He has made a deliberate act to choose our store over a big box department store. He has done all the research he could but now he is looking for advice and is ready to buy. In those days, the camera outfits were considerably expensive, and he needed to be sure he could trust us with his money, and so he would start to talk about what he was looking for. I would show him his options. And we would close the sale. And repeatedly, I was outselling the guys who chose to stand in the door. I was dumbfounded as to why they would let the actual buyer pass right by them. At the time I thought it was funny or maybe unusual and I had not quite put into perspective what was really going on.

The situation was greatly beneficial to me because not only did I maintain my status as the number-one seller in the state and receive a commission, while getting experience as a salesperson,

I also met my husband. So, the pay, the sales experience, and the husband have provided me with a huge return over the years. What I also did not realize was that it was preparing me for a career in corporate sales training.

Several years later I left high school teaching and began working in enterprise sales training. I found myself applying many of the philosophies that I had learned and employed as a teacher in the new setting. At that time there was a push to move from transactional selling to solution selling. It was the beginning of the Fourth Industrial Revolution with the addition of innovative technology and products daily. This meant moving from product-centric selling to solution selling. Also, the Internet and other technologies were appearing on the scene, and this was a lot to take in for both sellers and buyers. We based solution selling on what was keeping the CEO up at night. Even so, there was a sense that the customer was making an informed decision, but in reality, they did not have enough information to do that. They needed a knowledgeable partner to help them. This is not unlike the young man buying his first camera package back in the little store in New Hampshire.

Selling had been through many iterations by then. Often salespeople would say their product just sold itself. That works only when it is a one-of-a-kind item that just bedazzles the customer. But once there is a choice, then differentiating yourself becomes much harder. Add that to the impact of the Internet in terms of how we all get information and make decisions, and it was time for a novel approach. All this had a massive impact on the status quo. At that time, sales training was often delivered in a single event. Salespeople would attend a conference or attend training sessions in a boot camp. And training sessions were lecture based. They might even hear from an inspirational sales leader who basically told them to "be me and you will succeed like I did." This was the antithesis of everything I knew about training and knew about what made me successful in selling. And I was not the only one thinking that way.

Soon new sales methodologies were hitting the scene. Some of them such as SPIN Selling achieved remarkable success. This proved to be a stepping-stone to keep salespeople in line with the changing demands of the buyer. Insight selling followed, and it incorporated the notion that industry and market pressures might be keeping that CEO up at night rather than worrying about a product breaking down. Just to complete the picture we cannot discount the power of the Challenger sale, which focused on the buyer and the buying decision. Most salespeople these days have familiarity with these methodologies, but I still hear them say, "I don't need another methodology. I just need to close some sales."

These sales methodologies are powerful and have brought salespeople success. So why do we need yet another methodology? We must face the impact of the Internet on buying and selling. Buyers no longer need a salesperson to make a sale. Right now, you can buy anything from a bar of soap to an automobile online without any human interaction. This phenomenon was accelerated by the pandemic of 2020 that isolated us all in our homes with our computers. Since I have been working with those sales methodologies for years in terms of the sales training that I have been designing and developing, I have come to believe that these approaches kind of leave the salesperson hanging in mid-air once they make the proposal. So, I started thinking about a hybrid model that reflected this postmodern environment. In a way I was going kind of back to the future, looking at customer-centricity and thinking about the whole lifecycle of the buyer-seller relationship. In this world, salespeople must establish an authentic and supportive relationship. The seller must be a valued partner and therefore needs a sales methodology that supports it. It must be REAL, and that is how the REAL Sales Methodology was born. REAL is an acronym for Research, Engage, Advocate, and Lead to the Solution. This approach enables the salesperson to differentiate themselves competitively, truly and authentically, and keep their customers coming back for more.

I hope you enjoy this book. My hope is to ensure you are the number-one seller every week from this day on.

Chapter 1

WHO NEEDS A NEW SALES METHODOLOGY?

SALESPEOPLE SO OFTEN have built quite a reputation for themselves. You can imagine the kind of pushy used car dealer that's personified on television, smashing windshields with axes, having their children invite you to the dealership, and performing all kinds of gimmicks to get your attention. You can also imagine the highly consultative salesperson who almost becomes your best friend where you can talk about the ups and downs of life. And everyone remembers the adage, "No one ever got fired for buying IBM." These all form the mythology surrounding sales. Salespeople have a difficult job every day. It is a challenge with new demands on their time and pressure to close deals. You can imagine situations where salespeople are depicted almost as pawns to their business, being forced to meet that number. On top of that, if you've worked with sales either in training or as a manager, then you have likely seen them multitasking and described or even self-described as having a short attention span. If in trying to talk to them, I find they appear not at all interested, then how did I come to the conclusion that they need a new sales methodology, that I must introduce them to another way of approaching sales, and that they should be eager to internalize it and then insert it into their current practice?

Time for Some Myth-Busting

Having worked with salespeople for over 20 years, I am familiar with what they are really like and how that, in fact, differs from how they are perceived. I find that most of you in sales are very success-driven but at the same time risk-averse. That differs greatly from the perception that salespeople are coin operated and very selective. There are a lot of elements within the existing and historical sales practices that work and should be preserved. Additionally, the REAL methodology must take into consideration the fact that salespeople must perceive success immediately. They will want even the smallest success initially to prove the methodology will work overall. This new methodology will build on the success of those that have gone before and respond to the needs of today's seller and buyers.

So, let's just address the needs of the success-driven seller. Every conversation, every interaction, every moment that you are thinking about your customer or client, speaking with your customer or client, preparing something for them, or receiving something from them, you need to achieve some success to move your relationship forward. And every stage of the REAL methodology addresses this. I can't say that about every stage of every methodology that has come before. But I will guarantee that salespeople who are truly success-driven will easily align their approach to this methodology and achieve immediate success. Therefore, reinforcing that behavior and carrying it to the next stage is the desired outcome.

But I Don't Need Another Methodology!

Many of you might be thinking, "I just don't need another methodology. Thank you very much. I don't need change because I'm fine here, entrenched in my current process that is as comfortable as my fuzzy slippers." Sales is complicated and difficult. Don't get me started on my reaction to the term "soft skills" when selling is about the hardest skill to master. Just because sales is complex does not mean that the sales methodology has to be. The idea is to establish a methodology that returns frequent success milestones while addressing the complex needs of the long-term customer relationship. While the REAL methodology addresses the success-driven needs of the seller, it offers a familiar low-risk path aligned to the buyer. Change is not easy and often feels like a high-risk situation. The REAL methodology provides the framework for many familiar functions, and that's why I believe the combination of the familiar and the new will quickly feel like the aforementioned fuzzy slippers.

Business and sales leadership will tell you that their customers are demanding more. They see the need to be more consultative and less transactional. They are moving their company to a customer-centric mission, and the sales team needs to represent that change. They are wrestling with the impact of a worldwide pandemic that has driven buyers to change their behaviors sometimes at the expense of whole industries. It is time for salespeople to recognize their own superpower and actually become the competitive edge of their company. I have always believed that they could be, and that's what REAL Selling is all about.

TRANSACTIONAL TO CONSULTATIVE

When I was very young, I used to watch a show with my brother called *The Rifleman*. *The Rifleman* starred former-basketball-star-turned-cowboy-actor Chuck Connors as the sharpshooter Lucas McCain, the morally solid and strong widower who with his son Mark navigated the tough world of North Fork, New Mexico, back in the 1880s. And periodically they would travel probably by wagon to the mercantile, the general store, run by Millie Scott and Hattie Denton. The general store sold dress fabrics, salt, and animal feed. The thing was, the general store was kind of a social center where people would run into each other and greet each other in a friendly way. Even though the show was referred to as violent realism at that time, it did show a fairly realistic depiction of the way buying and selling, even in those days, was more than simply a transaction.

When you think of transactional selling, it pretty much sits in the retail environment. But even back then, that general store offered more. You can see in your mind's eye old Lucas and Mark heading in for some of those vital provisions. The general store was the source for almost everything from sugar to hair pomade, from fabric to stove polish. And before anyone would hand over their hard-earned coins to buy something, the first primary transaction would occur—the sharing and receiving of news. In the case of our friend Lucas McCain, he would have a carefully prepared list of what he planned to buy. But if he was lucky old Hattie might remember something he bought for last year's dry season, and she might suggest it to him. That one additional thing might be needed for the cold winter nights coming up over the horizon.

The moral of the story is that even though there are only a couple of elements of the old general store that apply today, there are a few key takeaways. On the surface, it looks like pricing items for sale and then collecting that price from a buyer was the whole story. It is not. Transactional selling is never enough. Even then the storekeepers were aware of their role in watching the buyer's back. If you really analyze that situation in the 1880s, you will note that it is likely that the reason the buyers came back every week was more for the news than the supplies. The transaction itself is fundamental to the sale. That's a given. But continuing with a purely transactional approach to selling is not the best way to get the most sales. I've already mentioned the exchange of news as being an important element of the general store experience. In a way this is akin to some of the relationship-selling or insight-selling techniques in the modern world.

The second piece of the general store experience that's so valuable is the customer-centricity. Hattie knows her customers. She knows what kind of candy stick little Mark likes when he comes in with his pa. She knows the kind of things that Lucas is going to need for the winter, and she's probably hyperaware that he's a widower and he doesn't have a woman at home to help him back in the kitchen. She's using that insight to guide the kind of conversations she has with him when he's in the store, offering things he might not be thinking of because of his situation. If she's really good, she's using some of those old Challenger techniques in how she talks to him.

Today's Buyer

Of course, in the 1800s, buyers did not have many options like they have today. These days people can pretty much look up whatever they want online, find it nearby or far away and at all different prices. If they have the time to search around and find it for the cheapest, they can order it there. If they need it right away then they might choose to pay more. They make that decision every day, so that means the burden is on you as a seller to be more than the product online. You must be the guy that's thinking about what that customer needs, thinking about how what you're offering might be of interest to them, and serving as a treasured partner. That's what we're really looking at here.

The funny thing is you can look at some enterprise sales teams and you can think, oh they're so modern and so consultative. They are using some of the most modern techniques. They know social selling and solution selling. They've been doing that for years. They know all about Challenger—who doesn't? They know exactly what to do to be a Challenger. They are using insight selling. They've done relationship selling, and they know SPIN Selling like the back of their hand. But the reality is, they are still going on a call with a new client and spending the whole time parading their products in front of them as if the product had the power to sell itself. And then they wonder why the client is kind of baffled or just wanders away and asks somebody else to show them something to compare it to. It's because what they're doing is a transactional sale, and it just doesn't fit in today's world. Even old Hattie could tell you that.

A New Approach

One of the biggest problems with a transactional approach is actually trying to find leads. The model of opening your store and displaying your storefront is not enough, even if your storefront is a website. Unless you get an engagement with somebody to show your product to, you really don't have anything to talk about. And that's why when we look at this new methodology called REAL Selling, we begin with the R which stands for research. It is the first step to getting to know your customer. Let's go back to the general store and examine the part where our little merchants Hattie and Millie were the most successful. It is when they were anticipating Lucas' needs and worrying about him. You could interpret that as recognizing his needs and enabling his success. On the surface it may seem like everyone has the same challenge out on their dusty old ranches when the wind starts blowing and the well has gone dry. Hattie and Millie make it personal. They make it their business to know what challenge Lucas faces. Millie says to him, "Well, last year you only bought this much, but you know from what I understand from some of the travelers that have come through recently it's going to be a tough winter. You know you might need to double that." When she's doing that, she's consulting. She's putting the customer first. She's thinking about the customer and aligning herself as a trusted and valued partner. She's leaving the shackles of transactional selling behind and spending time with that customer doing everything you ought to be doing in your sales conversations.

Can't I Get an App for That?

With all this talk of research and lead generation, you might be thinking, "Can I just get an app for that?" The easy answer is, of course you can, and his name is the Internet. As you know you can buy anything you want on the Internet, and the second you buy it or even search you will be inundated with cold calls in the form of ads in every website you look at. When you go to look for something, the website will offer you other things that are similar or other things that other people buy. It provides you with reviews from other clients and customers. It will ask you and then pester you to review what you buy. So, in a way, nobody needs a salesperson at all.

The reason to practice a new sales methodology is because replacing sales with an app is not a complete answer for your customer. An app can provide a lot to a buyer, but before you go thinking you are being replaced by your smartphone, you should consider your own special differentiation. Let's go back in time to the first iteration of Microsoft Office. If you opened a Word document back then and started to type, a little animated paper clip named Clippy used to pop up and state the following: "It looks like you are writing a letter." Then it would wait for you to answer so it could offer you help in your letter writing. It was probably put there to let you know that there were some templates available to use. The reality was that Clippy never was that helpful, and even now if you say to someone, "Oh, this is just like Clippy," they know exactly what you're talking about. It is a little paper clip that thinks you're writing a letter. Well, the same thing happens with the automation and app-based activity surrounding sales on the Internet. My personal favorite is that if I buy something, particularly something expensive, it will then inundate me with ads about the exact same thing that I just already bought. Bottom line is the app doesn't know any better.

The app doesn't know me. The app just knows people it thinks are like me and it's probably just looking at what I searched for, not what I actually bought. It also reminds me of the attempt at business intelligence by grocery stores when they started gathering information on what we were buying. They really didn't know how to use that information. They would churn out a bunch of coupons that really didn't have anything to do with what I was interested in. The reality is the salesperson brings not only additional knowledge to the table, but the understanding, the partnership, the care, the concern, the understanding of the business, and the desire for success for the client. An app just cannot do that.

You can put the customer at the center of a conversation without guessing. And once you start thinking about it, you'll be able to identify areas where a digital tool or app could help you. There are a lot of digital tools out there, but I can tell you right now the first answer is not an app. The first answer is always to understand your own process, your own need. So, for example, if you want to understand the market trends, you can use certain apps that make available access to data and news around those kinds of subjects. They can provide daily updates and alerts for industry news and access to resources. There are also apps where you can contribute, approve, peruse, and share your research. No matter how you use an app to support you, it still requires the magical "you" to connect the dots and prepare for that all-important customer conversation.

USE DIGITAL TOOLS FOR SUPPORT

A digital tool or app can only support your best practices. It cannot replace them. So often these days, people will turn to an app to solve a problem. We used to say, "If you are a hammer every problem looks like a nail." Now we can say that for people, every problem cries out for an app. I can recall the early adoption of one of these social-media platforms that the company I was working for bought in order to enable the sales team to access information. We spent a lot of time ensuring curated content was located in the various spaces and then headed out to train all the sales team on it. One feature of the platform was the ability to notify you if someone posted something. Before we rolled out the training, many of the salespeople decided they did not want the notifications and they configured Outlook so it would put the notifications in the delete folder. They did not know enough about the tool to appreciate its value and use it properly. Just automating a function because you can is not a reason to do it, and using it improperly may just inhibit your sales success rather than enhance it.

An area where there is something of an app explosion is in prospecting and lead generation. Many communication and research functions can occur using an app. My caution is that the key to the whole successful operation is still you. In order for you to use the information that a tool generates, you need to consciously engage with your prospect. A good example of this is LinkedIn. LinkedIn can be extremely useful to a salesperson as a representation of your capability and experience. It enables you to share your thought leadership and engage in the community as an expert. You can read the profile of the person you're going to meet with to understand a little something about them. And, frankly, it is a crime if you don't. People expect you to be interested in them. There are additional capabilities that LinkedIn provides including the ability to search for people who have left one of your client companies and could connect you to someone in their new company. This is a true prospecting opportunity. But it's not like you just log on to LinkedIn and it magically provides you opportunities. You must establish and maintain your own profile, understand the ways to use your postings, and participate in discussions.

Time to Get REAL

First, you should align to a methodology. In this case R for Research, E for Engage, A for Advocate, and L for Lead to the Solution—REAL Selling. Then you can put together a plan to support those steps with digital tools. Without a methodology and a plan, you end up with what I experience multiple times every single day. The phone rings. The phone is disturbing buyers with multiple calls every day. It is a robot calling who says, "Hello, this is Ralph, how are you today?" and if you say "fine" or anything like that, he starts rambling on about whatever he is selling. I generally just hang up, but the other day I said, "Ralph, are you a human?" and he answered, "There is a human behind this call, but it sounds like you're not interested so I'll put you on the do-not-call list." A robot is not a salesperson. If you were on that call with me, you would likely have been able to engage in a conversation and possibly make a sale. These stumbles are not exclusive to cold calls.

My favorite story about a failure in using digital tools properly is an e-mail that I was sent regarding a training development service. At that time, I might have been interested. So, they sent me an automatically generated e-mail that started out asking me if I knew what gamification in learning was. They used my name three or four times in the e-mail and told me I should really investigate it. When I did not respond, they sent me the same e-mail again. At that point, I was frustrated specifically because the salesperson was relying on these computerized e-mails rather than doing his own homework. I proceeded to light his inbox on fire to tell him that if he spent a millisecond on my LinkedIn profile, he would know that I had just published an article on gamification and learning in an industry magazine and I was actually considered to be a thought leader in this area. It had become clear to me that he didn't look at or even care about me. He just used a tool and believe me, he did not connect the dots. It's more like he created a trap for himself. The reality is, he might have verified me as a prospect if he had done a little homework and then engaged me based on where I was. You can see from this how you can easily misstep using some of these digital tools improperly.

A History Lesson

To fully grasp how we got to the REAL methodology, we need to take a stroll down memory lane and study the history of key elements of past methodologies and sales myths. Early on, salesmanship was believed to be solely a natural ability. You were either born with the innate ability to sell or you were not. In 1916, President Woodrow Wilson addressed the first World Salesmanship Congress in Detroit, saying, "There have been two ways of doing business in the world outside of the lands in which the great manufacturing has been made. One has been to try to force the tastes of the manufacturing country on the country in which the markets were being sought, and the other way has been to study the tastes and needs of the countries where the markets were being sought and suit your goods to those tastes and needs." This was quite the landmark quote at the time. At about the same time, D. M. Barrett, the editor of *Salesmanship Magazine*, published articles about trust-based selling and this notion of understanding the market's needs. Prior to that the myth that salespeople were born, not taught, meant that companies produced handbooks of tips, as Henry B. Hyde of the Equitable Life Assurance Society published in 1859. John Henry Patterson, the founder of NCR, based his approach on a 16-page handbook, *The NCR Sales Primer*, written by his brother-in-law, Joseph H. Crane. In 1893, Patterson headed to the World's Fair in Chicago to see how his salespeople were doing. When he quizzed them, he found they knew nothing. So, he rounded them up into a hotel and the first sales training school was born.

The school focused on what would be known as the Patterson Approach and its four steps with the goal to schedule a demonstration: <u>approach</u> to introduce yourself, <u>propose</u> to describe the cash register for the first time, <u>demonstrate</u> to carefully lead the customer to the point of purchase, and <u>close</u>. The salesman was not to move into the close phase until he was sure the merchant recognized the value of the cash register. Salesmen were encouraged to exert pressure in a forceful yet subtle way. They would remind salesmen "that no man likes to be sold to" so "avoid giving the impression that you are trying to force him to buy." The NCR methodology was based on sympathy toward the business interests of the buyer and sincerity in presenting the machines. Certainly, elements of what Patterson considered important are still important to this day. What he did not know was he was shattering the myth that people are born sellers and proving that sales methodology can be learned.

But just because Patterson started a sales training school does not mean everything was fixed. Over in Detroit, Henry Ford was adding his voice to Science in Selling. Science in Selling promoted phrenology as an alternative sales method with its ability to read a prospect's character by the shape of their head. Although this may sound bizarre, it was adopted by Ford Motor Company, which, in 1923, suggested seeking out customers with high foreheads who should be more imaginative and therefore better prospects. It wasn't until 1925 that the notion that people can be trained to be good salespeople would actually begin to take hold. From this stage, we can harvest the notion of training and methodology enabling successful selling. We also see the beginning of empathetic listening as a priority.

What Makes Buyers Tick

From the '20s through the '50s there was a focus on the psychology of selling—the goal was understanding how buyers tick. Understanding the psychology of selling was promoted by Dale Carnegie and the Ford Motor Company. Dale Carnegie was universally known for his insight into self-improvement through understanding personal behavior. His contribution to improving sales became what is known as relationship selling. He was a much-sought-after speaker and publisher from 1915 through the late '70s. This period emphasized the importance of understanding your customer and aligning your behavior to his.

In the interim years, several methodologies emerged, each with maybe one or two redeeming qualities. Barrier selling established a practice of asking leading questions where the answer would always be yes. This was the beginning of open-ended questioning techniques. Here begins the alphabet soup of sales methodologies. *SELL*—Show, Explain the Advantage, Lead to Benefit, and Let them talk—enabled the salesperson to show features while telling success stories. *ADAPT*—Assessment, Discovery, Activation, Projection, Transition—became popular in Britain in the 1950s. This method was something of a pseudo-technical assessment in hopes that the prospect would discover on their own how a product would benefit them. *ARC*—Ask, Recommend,

Cross-sell, Close—focused on asking the customer what they wanted and then introducing complementary items to increase the size of the order.

THE MODERN ERA OF SALES

From the late 1950s through the '80s, many standardized approaches bubbled up based on some fixed selling formula. The first real example of this was *Needs Satisfaction Selling*, developed by Xerox, to support their salespeople at the time that Xerox's patent on dry photocopying ended. It was based on the notion that no one wants to be sold anything, but they did want to make informed decisions. Helping the buyer in their decision-making process produced stronger worker relationships. This method was so successful that Xerox commercialized the concept and formed Xerox Learning Systems in 1972. The company promoted its methodology as Professional Selling Skills (PSS), which included other sales development programs such as speed reading, customer service skills, sales management, and interviewing skills.

In response to OPEC's grip on oil prices in the '70s, Robert Miller of Kepner Tregoe Consulting and Stephen Heiman, a former IBM salesman, introduced strategic selling. It enabled salespeople who had PSS skills to manage large and complex accounts. *SPIN Selling*—Situation, Problem, Implication, Need-Payoff, a consultative approach developed by Neil Rackham in 1988—followed. *SPIN Selling* is based on the formula to ask the right kind of questions, reduce the need to sell, discover the problem that is hurting the customer, rescue the customer by introducing certain products or services. This very popular approach is based on four different types of questions: Situational questions—discover the background—and Problem questions—uncover the hurt and by doing this early in the process, the trap is laid. The questions asked lead directly to the rescue: Implication questions—bridge the gap to the product or service—and Needs-Payoff questions, which give the customer something to identify how a solution would resolve the pain. The explicit need identified allows the seller to state the benefit. This is the infancy of a more consultative approach to selling.

In 1983, Mike Bosworth founded his company Solution Selling, and in 1993 he published *Customer Centric Selling*—a solution-oriented 8-step approach to sales. He was still focused on the product to some extent, but his emphasis on pre-call planning and research as well as techniques to stimulate interest still hold true to this day.

THE POSTMODERN ERA OF SALES

A lot was happening in the world in the following years. Technology was booming and information was exploding. This impacted both selling and buying. Historically, customers needed salespeople. Initially they needed salespeople to inform them because they had little access to information. They also had limited choice. Over the last century, but more particularly, over the last decade or so, the same customers have been overwhelmed with information. They don't need salespeople to provide information, they need salespeople to help them wade through the masses of available information to find the salient facts and identify the best fit solution. Although it may have seemed like the change started slowly, it really was more like a sudden earthquake. Solution selling and product-focused transactional selling would go the way of the dinosaur. Sellers needed a new approach. More than ever salespeople had to become more consultative, and they had to have skills to build trusted relationships.

You can see from the history so far that the formulae were getting more and more complex. In 2011 Brent Adamson and Matt Dixon published *The Challenger Sale: Taking Control of the Customer Conversation*. It was a landmark addition to the evolution of sales training. The approach included messaging from marketing that aligned to the process and empowered the seller to build strong relationships while challenging buyers to think differently about the future of their business. It required sellers to have unique insights about the market, the industry, and the seller. It enabled them to tailor themselves to the customer's specific needs and push back when necessary to take control of the sale. Adamson & Dixon saw the value in solution selling but put forth the notion that "Customers don't need you the way they used to." They contend that businesses have long understood their own problems, which is why solution selling worked, but now customers need valued partners to help them solve their problems. Selling has become much more complex.

There was a clear need to start selling differently. It had become more difficult for the salesperson to be an asset to the customer. This meant not just improving the sales technique but changing how they sell altogether. To be a change agent, the salesperson must be confident and knowledgeable about the customer's business. They can no longer just describe a great solution or serve as a friendly informant. The biggest change was to turn a customer with clearly defined requirements into one with emerging needs. A Challenger seller would say, "Here is everything you asked for in the RFP—but I think we should talk about what you did not ask for."

Challenger hit the selling world like a sonic boom. Many companies began changing their marketing approach, training their sales teams, and revising the stages of their sales cycle. There was a heavy focus on the persona of the seller and the persona of the buyers. The research behind the buyer's journey and other market trends powered the transition. It was a complex solution to a complex problem, and some sales teams just resisted it or stuck a toe in and decided the water was too cold. The truth is, Adamson & Dixon delivered a breakthrough event to the history of selling. After the book launched everything was, indeed, different.

So, was that it? The evolution of sales was over. Selling was now Challenger selling, and no one needed to introduce another methodology. Could that be true? Not by a long shot. Many authors and organizations began to ideate on the "next big thing" for selling. Several books appeared on the shelf called *Insight Selling*. They built on the understanding of the buyer from Challenger but took it a step further to build rapport with the customer as a trusted advisor, sharing insights with the buyer. Buying had become more complex, and often buyers struggled to figure out what they wanted or needed. They struggled to navigate the buying process and felt crushed under the pressure to "sell" their plan, project, or buying choice internally alone. They did not benefit from a one-size-fits-all approach. They needed someone to help them understand how to succeed at making the best buying decision. Sharing insights and stories power the conversation in these situations.

For 163 years, people have struggled to align the perfect sales methodology with the current buying trends. From the downright mind-boggling method of looking for buyers with big foreheads to Challenger sales and insight selling, we are still in need of a simple answer. By pulling the strongest threads from each approach, it all comes down to REAL Selling—Research, Engage, Advocate, and Lead to the Solution. Salespeople need a simple methodology to solve a complex problem.

Chapter 2

WHY REAL SELLING MATTERS

SELLING IS HARDER than ever. The impact of advancements in technology, social media platforms, and other communication tools has been tremendous both in a good way and a bad way for the salesperson. In one way, it has made new avenues available to communicate with clients and customers, but in another way we all feel rather beleaguered by the constant intrusion of phone calls, texts, advertising, and other cold-calling techniques in our lives. This has led to frustration on the part of the buyer and likely you as the seller. In addition, the global disruption of the COVID-19 pandemic has caused people to work differently and communicate differently. For some businesses that rely heavily on in-person sales, this has been a nightmare. That does not mean that people are asking for the next great sales methodology, but the most common methodologies are not enough.

There are many familiar and not-so-familiar methodologies out there in the world right now, and many companies are trying to discover the next big thing. I think we can all agree that often the existing method primarily focuses on prospecting and sometimes to making a proposal. Beyond that it often feels like falling off a cliff. It helps you—there is no doubt about that. If you follow the methodology, you can identify a customer, work with them to identify what the proper proposal is, and maybe even get them to sign it, but there is no methodology to support you beyond that. That is why the notion of the REAL Selling Methodology is so exciting.

REAL Selling for the Long-term

With the REAL Selling Methodology, you begin with the end in mind and plan for the long-term relationship with your customer. You become the differentiation for your brand. Your partnership is valued by the customer enough that they call you to buy the next thing. This methodology will support you through your longer-term relationship, and I don't just mean that you get the proposal and then say, "Do you want fries with that?" You should think of that first proposal as the first of many. As you offer insight to the customer, whether in a proposal or not, it represents your relationship and your interest in them. That is what is important and that's why they will come back to you again and again.

Research Builds Competitive Differentiation

How many times have you asked your marketing department or your manager for more competitive information? How many times have you wished you had that magic bullet that would just eliminate your competition forever? I say recognizing that you yourself are the competitive differentiation is an important step to true success in a long-term sales relationship. It's been said many times that people do not like to be sold to, but they do like to buy. Think about how you are helping them buy. This also aligns with the notion of the competitive differentiation you bring to your customers. They often experience difficult situations where they need help to accomplish their goals. In the old days we used to call this "the problem that keeps them up at night." These days we look at target areas where we can help them overcome a roadblock or challenge to their core business. By recognizing your potential return on investment for establishing yourself as a trusted advisor or valued partner, you will then reap the benefits competitively because the customer will recognize you as the value that they want. They will choose you over the competition because they value your insight and your understanding of them. This is really important, and it's the reason why the REAL Selling Methodology begins with the R for research. Research is the key to preparing for a conversation with your customer, getting to know them, getting to know what their company is all about, and what their company's plans are. Being able to align yourself in an authentic way that is recognized by the customer fuels the customer's confidence to continue to buy from you. More importantly, the customer will tell other people like them why they should buy from you. And that is your competitive differentiation in action.

Engage Your Customer Like It's 1899

One of my favorite stories of sales initiative is the Jell-O story. Jell-O, now a fruit-flavored powder-based gelatin, actually was developed back at the turn of the 20th century in 1899. A young man was trying to make some kind of sore throat elixir and ended up developing a gelatin and decided that it could be something. He wasn't sure of what and he ended up selling it for a grand total of $450 to another man. That was an enormous amount of money in those days. The other man worked on the invention and around 1904 added fruit flavoring and thought it would be a good dessert. I believe as the story goes his wife had some input into the flavoring decision. But in spite of it being a great idea it really didn't take off. People weren't interested in it, and they didn't understand it. He got very frustrated with the fact that people did not see his vision for it. He had partnered with Nico, the manufacturer, and he told him, as quoted from the Jell-O Museum website, "You can have the blankety blank thing for $35." Well, Nico had some ideas about what to do, although he had no idea his approach would become a marketing and sales legend. Nico decided to build his own demand.

He marketed Jell-O in two ways. First, he took what was then an enormous amount of money—$396—and bought an ad in the *Ladies Home Journal* that said that with Jell-O you could create the world's best recipes. Then he printed these recipe booklets employing some familiar artists to draw some of the images in the booklet, including American painter and illustrator Maxfield Parrish and some other names that might be familiar to you even to this day. They created all these Jell-O recipes, both desserts and salads. Some of them you might remember from your grandmother or great-grandmother from days of yore. The point is that he didn't go out and give samples of Jell-O or try to get people to eat it. He went door to door and gave out these recipe books. The only way that the people who got the recipe book, and at that time it was all women, could make any of these recipes was if they went to their local store and they bought a box of Jell-O.

Soon women everywhere were asking for Jell-O and the stores began stocking their shelves to meet the demand. Nico created his own market demand by giving out these recipe books and just saying they are the world's best recipes. In no time at all he turned his $35 purchase and small marketing investment into a $1,000,000 enterprise. And as you know you can go in and buy Jell-O today, more than 120 years later. Nico understood his target audience. He knew he had to get into the home, and he had to talk to the woman who would be making the Jell-O salad or the dessert. He supplemented the advertisement with the vital information they needed to use his product. Now what's interesting about that is that all happened in 1904. That's a long time ago, but it offers us a lesson in customer-centricity and in the importance of truly understanding the value of your product to your customer. Many marketers and sellers have not learned the lesson of Jell-O and Nico. You can witness on TV today very transactional commercials saying, "here's our product, look at our product, look how good it is, here's 100 good things about it, now go buy it." That has never been the way of Jell-O and right now there are 1,396 recipes on their website.

BECOME THE TRUSTED ADVISOR

Many times, sales training and then ultimately a sales presentation begins with the product. There are even people who believe that knowledge of the product is the most important aspect of selling. By now I am sure you are sensing that it is the customer that is the most important aspect of selling. This is the difference between advocating for the customer and being an advocate for the product. The easiest way to put this into perspective is to go into the nearest hardware store. You might see someone standing in the power tools section looking at the drills. Why should they be confused? There are signs and brochures all around describing the features of each different tool. There are also QR codes on each product so they can look up more details. Still, they are befuddled. It is not until one of the employees strolls by and says, "What are you trying to do?" that our buyer starts to recover from indecision. Nobody really needs a drill. What they need is a hole. And it was not until someone was willing to serve as their advocate that they could see the light at the end of the tunnel. Imagine how it might have gone if that employee had simply started rattling off details of each drill.

Lead to the Solution like Crown Royal

Fast-forward to today and think about the approaches to marketing and selling. Not everyone gets what Nico got back in 1904, but a few do. Some of my most favorite examples are of companies using modern sales techniques like insight selling and Challenger methodology. There's one in particular that I think about every day. It captures the REAL Sales Methodology to a tee. The television commercial is for Crown Royal whiskey. Crown Royal is a pricey, high-end whiskey that comes in a fancy velvet bag. It's quite lovely and posh. I'm a Scotch drinker myself so I can't say that I've tasted it, but I know people like to display its uniquely shaped bottle. Whether it's Scotch or whiskey, prices can range from tolerable to special occasion to "we're never going to afford that in our lifetime." In this case, Crown Royal is on the upper end and it's fancy. In this commercial a young man played by a Broadway actor most known for his roles in the award-winning musical *Hamilton*, comes out of the shop with this bottle of

Crown Royal. You barely see it at the beginning, and he interacts with the neighborhood, greeting a neighbor, helping one lady with a plant she's trying to hang up, saying hello to some guys on the stoop. He is friendly and, clearly, he is a trusted friend of the neighborhood. You actually see him reinforcing that trust in his community in the way he continues his little adventure. He finally gets to his house, bounds up the steps of the brownstone, and greets his mother with great love. To this point, we have not had much identification of the product. As he shows his mother his gift, you can see for a split-second that he has brought the bottle of Crown Royal for her. She opens it up and they have a glass together.

AdAge Magazine posted about this ad on Facebook and one person commented, "It is so easy to see that he is a beautiful man. But being handsome isn't why I love this Crown Royal Ad. He embodies everything that I admire in a person. He is friendly to all he meets. He is confident! He takes time to give his Mama love and is surrounded by friends. I would be proud to call him my son, my grandson ... my neighbor. Just a GOOD person. A kind person. Someone with values who also enjoys a good time with friends." How powerful is that message? It doesn't mention any of the features and benefits of Crown Royal. It makes it about the value of sharing a glass together. It really has nothing to do with how the product is made, what the features of the product are, or even what the benefits of the product are. It has to do with the value of the product to those interactions, and so as you're watching this, you're just thinking, I wish I was in a neighborhood like that. I wish I were meeting people like this. I'd love to meet that guy. I would love to share a glass of Crown Royal at his family dinner with his mother.

The Crown Royal commercial is a visual depiction of an

insight story that demonstrates value. So, what happens is that you are actually seeing the whole value play out and it's leading you to the solution without even telling you overtly what the solution is. "Lead to the solution" is the L in REAL Sales Methodology. Nowhere in the story does it say what the problem is or what is keeping you up at night. It does not define a problem to solve or ask how big your budget is. None of that stuff comes up, but you just know that the next time you go to the liquor store, you're going to take a second look at Crown Royal. That's pretty interesting. Take a moment and think about the power of that.

Why **REAL** Selling Matters

Think of the REAL Selling Methodology as a simple solution to a complex problem. The next four chapters provide a deep dive into each letter of the acronym. Each letter represents both a mindset or approach and a set of activities to move the sales cycle along while enhancing the trusted relationship with the customer. Research to build trust and share insight, Engage to listen with empathy and understand the customer's situation, Advocate for the customer's success, and ultimately Lead to the Solution.

Chapter 3

R Is for Research

"Nothing is more powerful for your future than being a gatherer of good ideas and information. That's called doing your homework."

— Jim Rohn, Entrepreneur & Motivational Speaker

To be a successful seller, you don't have to be the smartest person in the room all the time, but you do need to keep up with the conversation and at the same time offer value to your customer. That means research. In other words, doing your homework. Many of the methodologies in the past would focus your homework assignment on your product line. Knowing your product is, of course, very important to your success, but it is not the only homework assignment facing you. I would suggest that knowing your product is only about one quarter of the research that you need to do to prepare yourself for a customer call. Your research assignment falls into four categories: know your customer, know their industry, know their market, and then know your product. The real challenge you face is the never-ending flow of information available on these subjects. Clearly, the homework is never ending.

Know Your Customer

Your potential customers post a whole lot about themselves online. That makes your research a lot easier. Remember, the idea here is to really "get them." Think about it on a grand scale about their company and on a personal or micro scale about the individual you will be speaking with. Why does it matter? You show your intent to support their success by understanding their situation and their company. And intent is key to building trust.

Begin by researching their website. Here are some examples of quick research including simply finding and exploring your prospect's website. You can gain an understanding of what is important to them by looking at the news section. You should see recent press releases and possibly some videos or interviews. Next, I always like to scan what they have posted for job openings. Often, they describe the details about the way they work that might be important to you. And finally, and likely the most important treasure trove, is in an area usually called Investor Relations under "About the Company." Look for the latest annual report and the 10K. It is in these documents that companies describe their plans for the future of the company. These documents are forward-looking and give you an idea of the upcoming initiatives and high-level activities. You will get a feel for their culture, what they value, and why they exist. This can be vital to the success of future conversations.

You might find out that your customer's company is beginning a huge new initiative to make them feel like one company, and that might be an opportunity for you. They might also value industry insights and showcase a few in the report. You might be able to find more. Look for what is most prominent on their website. They might be focused on the future, technology, sustainability, or even the pandemic. And don't stop at the company level. Be sure to read your stakeholder's profile on LinkedIn. It is critical to know what they have highlighted as important about themselves. I used to have a manager who said, "If you cannot solve the small problem, solve the bigger one." It was years before I could truly comprehend what he meant by that. Getting the big picture puts your planned conversation in context. That often applies to prospects because they are usually operating under some bigger umbrella. If you know about it then it just might open some doors for you. Between LinkedIn and their website, you should get a solid start at understanding the customer.

Know the Industry

In this day and age, you have to fully understand the industry of your customer. This means more than just knowing that truckers drive trucks on the highway, or that manufacturers need shipping labels. It also means more than recognizing the value of your customer's products to their customers. It's a given that trucks provide us with everything that we need to live, and that includes food, water, medical supplies, and more. In the past, you might have been given messaging about this industry that the whole goal was something called uptime. Clearly, the concept is important, but to truly know what the pressures in the industry mean, you must recognize that the trucking industry is a critical success factor for the health and safety of all people of the world. Uptime does not just mean that trucks are on the road. It means that medical supplies arrived safely at the hospital and fresh produce got to the market. Understanding the industry means you can also confidently discuss the various pressures and market trends that impact your customers every day. By recognizing and thoroughly understanding those pressures and trends, you will be able to craft conversations that will explore your customer's need for value and ultimately increase your sale.

Don't stop at just being able to talk about some of the trends. Link the trends to the future success of your prospect's company. Tie their business goals to the trend in the market. One example of a market trend impacting companies all over the globe is the change in consumer-buying practices due to the pandemic. Literally overnight, consumers went from shopping in brick-and-mortar stores to buying everything online. That meant that the products were actually distributed to the wrong locations. Instead of being in a distribution center for home delivery, they were on store shelves. And there were no shoppers in those stores.

Another trend that occurred recently is that due to the pandemic, quarantine requirements, and layoffs, several forms of financial assistance were put in place by the government in the U.S. This included a weekly $600 added to unemployment benefits and the American Rescue Plan child tax credit sent monthly to families. Because people quarantined at home, they delayed purchases and actually built up a surplus of discretionary dollars. All this meant a shift in how people spent money on consumer goods and an increase in the money they had to spend. Ultimately, it brought the supply chain to a grinding halt.

By understanding the trends, you can take a look at what the individual customer's needs are. One of the biggest factors in all buying situations is money. Everything costs money, sometimes a lot of money, and, therefore, saving money is really important to your customer. So as a market trend changes, or an industry pressure occurs that causes something to cost more money, your customers will be looking for ways to save money or become more efficient at what they're doing.

Think about those trends that were mentioned above. They represent pressures on the business. Those pressures result in issues and concerns that your customer must address. No need to ask what keeps them up at night. You already know that. It is literally what keeps you up at night thinking about your customer.

INTENT IS YOUR SUPERPOWER

Some sales training might suggest that you just simply mirror the persona that you see in the customer. That might appear to work, but establishing an authentic partnership is better by building trust and offering solid evidence of your intent. Your intent is to help your customer succeed by buying your product. That may sound complicated at first, but because it's grounded in your knowledge of the buyer's journey, their market and industry pressures, along with your deep knowledge of your own products, you will be able to lead them to a long-term partnership that will result in many sales.

Research does not occur only externally. You must use your discovery time with the customer to prompt lots of discussion and opportunities for empathetic listening. You must be authentic, and you must probe with questions to understand their intent, being honest with them in your responses. So, looking at your customer through the lens of a persona will help you accomplish that. In all my sales training I always start with the triad. The three things. Companies only do three things—save money, make money, and stay out of jail; that last one is just a lighthearted way of saying that they stay in compliance with the law, report their financials properly to their stakeholders and the government, and pay their taxes. But the truth is, in any company, some create projects and have the money to execute on them, some people implement the projects efficiently and try to save money for the company, and then somebody, usually the CFO, keeps the whole thing on track and in line with the rules. That means reporting structure matters.

Let me tell you a story. For about five years I worked for a SaaS company up in Detroit—well north of Detroit in the gentrified suburb of Troy. If you know Detroit, then Troy is at about 16 Mile. Anyway—super cute place, Starbucks every 5 feet, Panera in between a Bonefish Grill on every corner. And an Embassy Suites in the parking lot of the Tower where my company was located. Now if you know the Embassy, then you know they have a daily happy hour. And this one actually gives us three free drinks a night. So naturally, when I was there, I spent a little time in the lounge and usually had my dinner there. So, on this particular night, I was sitting at a high-top table that had three stools on each side. I was by myself working on my laptop, minding my own business, when here comes the three sales musketeers who plop down across from me.

They get their Maker's Marks and start jabbering about the end of the quarter and how they need to close deals, swearing up a storm and acting all blow-hardy. I was doing my best to ignore them. Then the one guy, the loudest, tells everyone to look at the e-mail he just got from "that woman CFO." I am trying not to roll my eyes. Anyway, he reads out loud her one-line message, "I have seen the demos and heard the pitch, but it all comes down to trust."

Now the guy yells out in rather colorful terms, "Just sign the paper, lady." Then he tells us what he plans to write back to her: "I have been in this business for 15 years and I know what I am doing." And he goes for 100 words about how great he is. Well, I bet you can imagine what I was thinking at this point!! So, I just slowly looked up from my laptop and said, "That isn't what she wants to hear." Well, that stopped them in their tracks. And they looked at me and said, "What do you know about it?" So, I said, "You guys are software salesmen, right?" They were like, "How do you know that?" I said, "Well, I am responsible for sales training for a software company." So, then my new smug best friends said, "Teach us something!" So, I said, "Companies only do three things—save money, make money, and stay out of jail. The 'save money' people are like procurement, the 'make money' people are marketing and sales, but the 'stay out of jail' people are your CFO there. And jail isn't necessarily prison. It is the two weeks she is stuck with the auditor at the end of the year reconciling the books. She wants to be assured that she can trust your software to keep her out of auditor jail. So, all you need to do to get her to sign is close that gap, baby! Tell her you understand how critically important her data is and then tell her the story of your customer who used to spend the first two weeks of July in auditor jail but once he got your software, he was flipping burgers on the beach with his family because he just pulled those reports and handed them over." Well, they bought me a drink and headed out to dinner. But the point is, they were not thinking about what was driving or stalling their customer. They just thought louder was better.

Considering your customer in terms of how their project or need supports the business of their company will help you provide insight and communicate your intent to help your customer succeed. And the requirements for insight change as the internal role of the stakeholder changes. In other words, the market trend may be the same, but your "save money" people may have a different take on it than the "make money" marketing or product development people. You must always research enough to support a powerful and compelling conversation that is meaningful to the individual and supports the behavior and business requirements of the company.

Putting Customers in Perspective

So, let's put this into perspective. There is a political map behind any proposal that helps you understand the organization of your customer. This is where you sort out who is who in the company and how they work with each other. It allows you to determine who must sign off on decisions, who might block decisions, and who will carry your message internally. Alongside of this is your success plan. Begin early in conversations to gather business goals and the intended behavior change your prospect is looking for. Remember, it is not what your prospect needs to know about your product, it is what they can do with it. By using a success plan, you can identify early who some of these players are, and what they truly think your product is going to do for them.

Let's start with the procurement or purchasing client. So many times, they are really in an ivory tower, often isolated from the business. They can get very bogged down in process with layers of middle management. They can also get wrapped in bureaucratic red tape. Because they are in the "save money" category, they rely on other departments to fund and qualify their projects. That is a good-news/bad-news situation. In one sense, there is always enough or more money if they can justify it. Bad news, though: it is probably use-it-or-lose-it money. That means they may have requirements to spend money within a certain quarter or year. If you put that quandary all together you get a person who is in the present and the future at the same time, trying to build a reputation for quality return to all internal clients and managing money against business justification and financial best practice.

The best way to be a valued partner is to brainstorm ideas with them both for the current project and possible future projects. They are not just fishing but they really want advice. They need you to help justify their projects. They must go it alone either by educating their manager to carry their flag or go before the leadership themselves. This is where giving the stakeholder a thorough understanding of our approach to the success plan so they can talk about it internally is so important. And finally, we need to make them the hero of the story even as we have conversations beyond their department.

We have talked about people in finance and procurement roles. Let's consider other roles in a business you might be engaging with. Sometimes your point of contact comes from marketing or a specific business unit. They are deadline specific, and content driven. By that I mean that they usually have some outcome they are driving toward, often with great urgency. They may not be fluent in the jargon of your product. What might surprise you is that they may not have a clear picture why there is urgency or what the specific metrics are. The thing about them is they have the money. They create the projects and provide the funding. This is why they rely so heavily on you to guide and educate them on the success plan and how it will support the goals of their company.

You might be selling to the sales department. Now, sales is in the "Make Money" category and they make ALL the money, so they have a lot of influence in the company. They also have all the horrible pressure to exceed their targets, so it is pretty serious business. Getting them to consider what they want salespeople to do, to say, to know, to show is the challenge. You will only be asked to build what they plan to implement. That means you need to be clear on your value and focused on their goals. They may have a lot of baggage that gets in the way of new technology. They are fueled by metrics so there is definitely fodder for a success plan that will appeal to them. Sales looks to you for solutions. They rely on you to craft easy-to-implement and effective solutions without bogging them down in the details. They will demand measurable metrics, especially business results. They will need many updates and status reports with the possibility of presenting to the C-level executives. The biggest trick of this group is that they want it all and they want it yesterday.

Up until now the focus has been on business-to-business-type customer preparation. Understanding your customer is important no matter what your sales structure is. It is more than just taking a walk in their shoes. It goes back to understanding the market trends and pressures they are under and then aligning those with the value of your product. Value is not the same as features and benefits. Look at it this way—the features of a product represent *what* and they can usually be found in the documentation or owner's manual; the benefits are the *why* and you will often find five or six items listed. But that is not enough to make the sale. It is your job to understand the product and understand your customer well enough to craft value statements specific to their needs. The value statement should begin with "the customer can." Here is an example. A pod-based coffeemaker is designed to brew a single cup of coffee in minutes. The features are five cup sizes, a 75-oz water reservoir, less than one minute brewing time, ice beverage setting, and small counter footprint. The benefits are it offers hot water on demand, offers a variety of flavors and programmable strengths for coffee. The value, however, is specific to your customer. Ask yourself, what can my customer do differently if they get one of these coffeemakers? They can provide a variety of beverage choices for guests without having to buy full bags of coffee beans. They can get a cup of coffee in under a minute. No more dirty coffeepots.

You need to be agile in these conversations; as I always say, *Be the Willow*—if you are a birch, your branches will break in the winds of change. Don't ever suggest that their projects are a moving target even though it feels like they are. You must be flexible in time and scope as features of new products are added or dropped or messaging changes occur, or something weird happens in the market or the boardroom and everything is changing. Therefore, research is key to your success.

R Is for Research: Thought Generator

Some ideas to noodle on prior to meeting with your prospect or customer:

1. When researching their website, do you have a clear picture of their mission statement or value proposition? What is their top priority?
2. What are the big bets for strategy highlighted in their annual report? Any plans to expand, downsize, consolidate, etc.?
3. What is the biggest industry-related headline? Consider both the good news and the bad news in the market.
4. Who is their competition? How are they different?

Chapter 4

E Is for Engage

"When the customer comes first, the customer will last."
— Robert Half, Founder of Robert
Half Employment Agency

THE RELATIONSHIP BETWEEN a salesperson and the customer has been described in many ways over time. For REAL Sellers it is important to think about that relationship as an engagement. The word *engage* means to be involved in or take part in something. The use of this word is to emphasize the business partnership that actually occurs between you and your customer. To this point we've talked about researching to understand your customer, their industry, the market trends, and your product, but now we need to focus on the actual method to engage with them in an authentic way.

Many times, a sales trainer or a sales guru will suggest that you need to earn the right to have a conversation with your customer or prospect. While this may be true, it has an adversarial tone which is quite different from a truly customer-centric approach. People like to feel respected, and they want to be able to trust you. In considering how to engage with your customers, it is important to examine your level of customer-centricity, your ability to build trust and handle objections confidently.

Being customer-centric rather than product-centric starts with having a clear understanding of what makes every customer unique. Communication, whether in person, on a videocall, on the phone, or in e-mail, forms the backbone of the relationship with your customer. Build trust and use empathetic listening to identify the customer's intent, and then lead them to the sale rather than lead with the products and demos.

You Need a PAO!

Certainly, your history with sales methodologies has enabled you to establish engagement with prospects and customers. Those practices and skills form the foundation of any successful communication. The truth is that authentic engagement requires both emotional factors like empathy and practical factors such as a call plan. Let's go back to basics. Having a clear agenda, either documented or in your head, will guide your conversation and ensure you cover all the necessary points. This can begin with the meeting invite. Include a PAO—a statement of Purpose, a list of Agenda topics, and then your intended Outcome. The beauty of this strategy is that it begins your conversation before you even engage with the prospect. Often, they will answer back and expand or refine the scope of your meeting. Most sales organizations have a defined opportunity evaluation process. To align to that, ensure you have a checklist in mind to help you structure every communication to achieve the highest return.

Focus on the issues of the customer. What is on their mind? You may even suggest some market pressures or concerns that you think might be influencing them. This is a good way to begin your engagement with them. For example, the pandemic of 2020 has affected just about everybody in their business life and in their home life. It is very likely that it's affecting your prospect in some way. This could be a good place to start. And it's not just important to identify what those issues are, but also find out what the priority is to address them. The best way to do this is to let them dump their bucket. Some of the items that are issues for them right now may not be something you can address, but as a valued partner even listening to them can improve your engagement with them.

Once they have identified the problems or issues that they are facing, it's important for you to ask them how they define both the challenge and the success. What are the outcomes that they're looking for? Don't just look to the future but ask them what they're measuring now. What are the metrics they are currently measuring, and what metrics would they like to measure in the future? This is a true opportunity to show your value and engage with them. Help them understand how to set achievable goals and then measure those results. Thinking about this at the front end of the deal is a much more effective way for you to succeed for the long-term with this customer.

As you engage with your client, you should focus on the impact your solution might have on them or their company. The way to do this is to get a full understanding of their current state and then also ask about their future state. What do they measure now? Is there a business metric that they currently track? Do they have a Net Promoter Score (NPS) they would like to influence or a customer satisfaction survey that is important to them? I like to ask, "What do you want your people to say, to know, to do, that's different from what they're doing now?" This could align to software that you're selling or another type of deal. This could relate to a consultation that you provide. The main goal is to explore with your client or customer what they are looking for in terms of business or behavioral impact. Most of the time, everyone wants to save time or save money, but you must dig into the details and uncover those metrics. Usually, you are selling against the status quo and comparing your solution to continuing without you. Setting measurable outcomes becomes a promise of value. The goal here is to define what success will look like and then prepare to come back, check on the progress of your promised value, and then you can go in for the expansion sale, cross-selling and upselling.

Your final piece of this puzzle is understanding the constraints. What has held them back from doing something about their problem already? Consider constraints in both directions—those constraints on the client side but also potential constraints on your side. This is about engaging the client in an authentic conversation about those roadblocks and challenges that lay ahead.

Remember that in a business context the word *problem* really translates to *pain*. The customer is experiencing a type of pain, and any positive result is actually a gain, whether it is saving money on gas because of improved mileage or using software to manage procurement more efficiently to accomplish goals in a very short amount of time. Whether you are holding a full conversation or having a short interaction with a customer, think about this formula:

Listen to hear exactly how your customer describes their situation.

Soften with a question in order to engage rather than simply answer. Here is an example: "Sure, I could talk for several hours on the subject, but I bet that is not what you want to hear. Do you mind if I ask … ?" Asking a question without a softening statement may feel abrupt and harsh, so wrapping your questions in this type of statement helps demonstrate your interest and builds trust.

Move the conversation to hear more about the results they are looking for. This is your chance to understand the intent, the greater goal.

You Need a LOU

Documenting your communications enables you to establish understanding on where you are with the customer and what the history is of your relationship. This will help you craft appropriate communications in the future. The key to all communications whether in person, in writing, or in a voicemail should reflect your deep understanding of their needs. You may have heard of a LOU—letter of understanding. This is a method to follow up every communication with an agreement about what was discussed. It also enables you to make every conversation personal. At first glance, it may seem like a thank-you note, but really it establishes documentation of an agreement to what you heard and what the next steps will be. You are following up on what they require but because it is an e-mail, you are establishing a "paper trail."

Using e-mails to document your communications works well

if you run into a roadblock or objection. In your conversation, acknowledge that there is a challenge, ask questions for better understanding, and work with the customer to resolve it. Then follow up with an e-mail to state your understanding of the issue and the proposed next steps.

Many books have been written on communication techniques, and they all likely provide some gem or hint that improves your effort in this arena. My approach to communication is the recognition that you are a valuable participant in a long, ongoing conversation. You must remember what was said before, what to focus on in the future, and take responsibility for your message. By that I mean, you must be able to do more than just say the words. Tell a story that conveys the message.

In your communication, whether in person, on the phone, or by e-mail, remember that metaphors and stories are powerful communication tools. Take all your knowledge of the market, the industry, and your products and combine it with your ever-growing knowledge of customer situations to build stories and metaphors to help make your case. As a core competency, storytelling will help you reframe the conversation. Including a story or metaphor represents your understanding of them and also works to endear them to you.

TRUST

Have you ever walked away from buying something and wondered what stopped you? It is likely because you just did not trust the situation. Or maybe the opposite happened, and you are wondering why you were so willing to make a purchase so quickly. The likely factor was trust. In a high-trust environment, everything can move very quickly. In a low-trust environment you might question everything, and that slows you down. This is called the trust tax. In the book *Speed of Trust* by Stephen MR Covey, he says, "Trust isn't a quality you either have or you don't, it's a learnable skill. Teams and organizations that operate with high trust significantly outperform those who do not cultivate trust at the core of their culture." When we trust people, we have confidence in them. When we don't, we are suspicious.

Why is trust so important? What do high trust and low trust look like? The higher the trust, the easier for the customer to understand you, and even want to buy from you. And trust is not something that just exists, it is actually a learnable skill. With practice, you can experience the importance of building a high-trust environment, avoid the trust tax, and continually foster trust. Think about the retail stores and customer support calls you like to work with, that you visit again and again. You will return again and again to a store you trust. You believe in the quality of its offerings and the validity of its pricing. The same is true for the service support lines. You will remember vividly the calls where you felt heard, and that the customer service representative really cared about you. You will avoid the one that did not listen. At the heart of that relationship is trust. One of the most important drivers of trust is character, and at its heart is intent. Do you really understand your customer? Do you listen and truly hear what they are experiencing? In many ways it is simply treating people the way you want to be treated. Make the qualities of high trust your strength. It will increase sales and more importantly develop repeat customers.

So, let us break it down. The two key factors are character and competence. Let us look at the two key components of character—integrity and intent. Think of integrity simply as honesty. That concept takes us back to the basics to be truthful to ourselves and to others. Practicing the ability to recognize and show intent is a worthwhile exercise. Use conversations with customers to understand their intent, particularly their long-term goals such as expanding their own business. By recognizing and appreciating their intent, you build trust with them, and they will look to you for advice and more sales. The second component of trust is Competence. Think about your own capability, including your knowledge of the customer, their business, and the products. That capability increases trust. Additionally, your past results reinforce this area.

So, what if the trust level remains low? Obviously, you pay a "tax"—one that Covey calls the trust tax. In a high-trust environment, things move quickly, the sale closes quickly, and expensive do-overs and returns are fewer. That is the heart of the trust tax. In a low-trust environment, the customer may not believe you or misunderstand and you will have to repeat or engage the manager. So, in a low-trust environment you pay the trust tax in time and money.

Think about character as a combination of honesty and the recognition of intent, and competence with your own capabilities and results; avoid the trust tax and you will be successful at establishing the high-trust environment that fosters more and faster sales.

Handling Objections

Engaging with your customer means more than building trust. Once you have achieved that, you may find your prospect or customer articulating objections or raising concerns. This should be considered good although it might feel bad. Why is it good? It is good because they trust you enough to share their feelings openly and honestly. It might feel bad because no one wants to hear complaints or objections. There are three things to remember about handling and therefore overcoming objections. First, an objection is a natural and expected part of the sales process. Some people even say that selling doesn't begin until the customer says no. Another important thing to remember is that the objection is not about you. Don't take it personally. Take it as an opportunity to move the sale forward. This is where your research becomes so important. Take time to think about the objection and how it relates to what you know about the customer, the industry, and the market. To overcome an objection, you have to know the actual objection, which is often different from the stated objection. This goes to our building of trust where we understand the persona and the intent of the customer. So, don't just hear the words and try to respond to the words, but listen for the meaning and probe for more details so you really understand exactly what the objection is.

Listen carefully to the objection, make eye contact, and work to understand. Acknowledge and empathize with the stated objection. For example, "I know what you mean. I've had a similar experience." Ask at least two probing questions. Be delicate. You might begin your question with "Do you mind if I ask you another question?" Summarize what you've heard. Confirm with the customer that you have a clear understanding of what their complaint or objection is. Then answer any objection and compare and contrast two options if possible. In other words, respond to what the complaint or objection is, but begin in a negotiation stance by offering two alternative solutions. You can try this, you can try that. And then confirm when the objection is resolved. Ask the customer if they feel more comfortable with this answer than before. Then you can close the sale. The truth is, if you have established a high-trust environment even if the answer is bad, even if the news is bad, your customer will support it because they understand that you have the very best intent in mind and that you're just trying to help them.

Many sellers fear facing objections from their prospects and clients. Assume you can handle any objection or complaint. Work to negotiate a solution by asking questions, probing for more understanding of their intent or purpose, and focus on the value. In the book *Everyone Sells!* by Lee Dubois, he identifies five ways to answer a question. Reverse it, explain it, admit it, deny it, or ask why. So, let's look at how you might answer a complaint about the price: "This widget costs more here than it does anywhere else."

Reverse it: "Is it worth more to you to receive the no-hassle warranty and peace of mind knowing our company is behind you with more than 800 locations?"

Explain it: "We provide a no-hassle warranty, which means more hours of use for your investment. The real benefit to you is the peace of mind knowing that we are behind you at more than 800 locations."

Admit it: "That's right, and it's worth the price considering that it's backed by our no-hassle warranty."

Deny it: "I would argue that you get much more for your money with this widget when you consider how you will experience more use and have the peace of mind knowing that it's backed by the no-hassle warranty."

Ask why: "Do you mind if I ask you a question? Are you shopping here for the lowest price? The price here reflects the highest-quality product, of course, but also the best warranties so you can ultimately enjoy more quality use."

Customer-centricity

To engage your customer, you must take a customer-centric approach, which enables you to hold more robust conversations leading to greater sales and better customer retention. Consider yourself a trusted advisor rather than a seller. A trusted advisor teaches, shares information, and then leads with the customer to the solution, enabling the customer to think about the big picture. Your customers run a business on a very tight timeline; downtime matters a great deal to them. They value their products very much. Put your customer at the center of everything and you will find that you will be much more successful.

Remember that value is not the same as benefits or features. Every product has the set of features and those are important. Think about it as the definitions found in a manual. They do not communicate value. Each of the features of a product is associated with a function that provides a benefit. Benefits are essentially generic. The product feature provides that benefit with or without the customer. But when you talk about value, you're talking about what the customer can do because of the features and benefits. So, it isn't like you can just drop the mic when you say a benefit. You have to convert that benefit into a customer-centric statement. As a trusted advisor and valued partner, you are putting the customer at the center of the value. It is the "why it matters" of the product. To say: "you know if you do it this way, you are going to get a measurable return." This can be anything from a savings at the gas pump to an acceleration to productivity. In other words, you turn the benefit into something specific that the customer can do because of that product. That's the value to the customer. Put the conversation in the context of customer value, and you will be able to sell more and provide more value to your customer, resulting in more sales and more customer loyalty.

E IS FOR ENGAGE: THOUGHT GENERATOR

Some ideas to noodle on prior to meeting with your prospect or customer:

1. What is your purpose for calling on your prospect? What outcome do you anticipate for the meeting?
2. What action items will you track following your meeting? What expectations do you have for yourself and for your customer? Have you defined your intent?
3. How will you handle objections and pushback? How are motivations and intent impacting how your prospect handles roadblocks?
4. Can you clearly define the difference between a product-centric presentation and a customer-centric one?

Chapter 5

A Is for Advocate

> *"Great salespeople are relationship builders who provide value and help their customers win."*
>
> — Jeffrey Gitomer, King of Sales, Author and Speaker

REAL SALES METHODOLOGY gives you a framework to leverage your previous learnings and experience and literally take your selling to the next level. You are familiar with solution selling, insight selling, and quite possibly Challenger selling. As you have progressed through your own selling experience with its roadblocks and victories, you have likely retained what works best for you. Applying those elements to serve as an advocate for your customer is the next phase of REAL. Notice that you are advocating for the customer, not your product or solution. It is the value to the customer that matters.

When we talk about commercial teaching in the Challenger model, we use the terminology Teach, Tailor, Take Control. Thinking of yourself more as a teacher rather than a seller will help you understand how schoolteachers often go into selling situations and can easily sell things partly because they're trained to listen for the needs and then respond emotionally to the person. Remember my story in the preface of working on commission after I taught school all day and being recognized as the top seller every week.

Each portion of teach, tailor, and take control is focused on the customer and enables you to be their advocate. Think about what is involved with Teach. It means listening more than you talk. It means asking open-ended questions. It means building trust and rapport. To do that you have to demonstrate your capability, your intent, your character, your integrity. It is quite emotional. When you think about that Tailor part of the process, you must realize it involves a high level of knowledge of your products, but you should not consider pitching your products just yet. You must understand your competitive positioning, and the true value to your customers. You must craft it all into a story, and the story needs to mean something to that specific customer.

You must be able to ensure that the story that you're telling will resonate with the person that walked into the store or that you scheduled time to meet, and not just a generic anybody. And then the "take control" piece is when you show them the bad side of sticking with their status quo, and in some cases this could be negative, especially when you explain the emotional impact. By taking control you will be able to lead them to the new way forward, which is your solution.

Dwight Shrut Knows His Customer

The television show *The Office* aired in the United States from 2005 to 2013. It depicted a very odd team of people who worked for a paper company in Scranton, Pennsylvania, called Dunder-Mifflin. There is an episode in the third season (Episode 13) called "The Traveling Salesmen" where the elder statesmen of the sales team pair up with the young first-time sellers and head out on sales calls. Of course, the show itself is a comedy, and obviously the situations are designed for laughs.

Naturally, one of the salespeople who is in her fifties is paired with a young saleswoman. The first thing they do is go to the hairdresser, who styles their hair in a very 1960s bouffant style. It is over-the-top and certainly something that the younger seller cannot fathom. When they get to the office of the client, we can all see a family picture on the desk. The wife and three daughters all have the exact same hairstyle. Now, obviously, when you are advocating for the customer, I am not suggesting that you style your hair to look like your prospect's. I am suggesting you search for and watch this particular episode of *The Office*. I believe it is something that will resonate with you.

The scenario that has always stuck with me the most is the one where the main and eccentric character Dwight goes to a customer who is planning to leave Dunder-Mifflin and go to a competitor. A very young, ambitious seller has been partnered with Dwight. This young seller says he knows exactly what to say with this client and that he will handle everything. Dwight agrees, although you can tell he is skeptical. While the young buck describes all the features and benefits of working with Dunder-Mifflin, Dwight reaches across the client's desk, picks up the office phone, and turns it around to face him. He dials a number, putting the call on speakerphone, and we can hear the hold-music playing. The music just plays on and on. By now both the young salesperson and client are starting to wonder what Dwight is up to. Every now and then he would glance over at the phone but continue somewhat relentlessly with his pitch until the customer finally turns to Dwight and asks, "What exactly are you doing?"

Dwight hangs up and explains that he had called the competitor's helpline. "You know that when you call us, someone will answer the phone and speak to you. It doesn't seem like anyone is interested in talking to you at the competitor's company. If this is the kind of wait for help you want then go with them, but if you want someone to listen to your concerns and give you an immediate answer, then we have everything you need." It was a dramatic sales lesson, and ever since I first saw the episode, I have not forgotten Dwight's demonstration of customer value. It is a great example of advocating for the customer. The young salesperson was giving a pitch he could have given to anyone anywhere, but Dwight focused on the one factor that mattered most to the customer and homed in on the value that he would appreciate.

When we talk about advocate, we are not talking about advocating for your solution or advocating to sell more products, we are talking about being an advocate for your customer's success. A customer may be worrying about what their business is doing or what success looks like. You should ensure that your conversation places them and their concerns at the center. Ensure that you provide them value as they share vital information with you to support your business case. That give and take of value is so important in the early stages. Demonstrating your intent as an advocate for the customer is a critical message for them to internalize. Take a lesson from our friend Dwight from *The Office*. Here, he was simply demonstrating the difference between his approach to customer service for this client and that of the competition. Of course, the scenario was built for laughs and entertainment, but the lesson is legitimate. Without saying the words, Dwight was demonstrating that he knows what the client needs. That's the way you must think about advocating for the customer, especially as you get further and further along in the sales cycle. The advocacy becomes more and more important.

MAKE IT EASY TO BUY FROM YOU

Fundamental to that approach is the notion of commercial teaching. This approach differs greatly from solution selling or death by discovery, where they come in, "I'll guess what you need," then "I'll tell you all about it, you'll buy it, and I'll leave." That approach does not work in the long term and does not scale with the business. Often you tell them about it, they ask questions, and then they start searching for the lowest price and leave before buying.

Most often buyers think they know what they want, but they really don't. To make it easy for buyers to buy, you should think about all the hurdles and roadblocks they must navigate in order to make the decision. To you the decision may seem easy because you have the perfect product and here it is. They should just recognize that and sign on the dotted line. But in reality, they're not visualizing your product; they're visualizing what their future is like with your product. So, by talking to them about that vision and helping them see how the product will benefit them, they will be able to make an easier decision to buy.

One of the most important tools you have in your toolbox is your knowledge of their world. This is what we call sharing insights. Insights take the form of stories that demonstrate to the customer, in a more personal way, what that value looks like to them. These insights should be based on a combination of knowing your customer segment, knowing the customer industry, and knowing the customer personally, combined with thorough research of the market trends and pressures. Some of the segments tend to value lower cost, but usually a sale can be positioned as a return on investment rather than a straight bottom-line low cost at the outset. That should be an easy conversation for you to have. Explore those industry insights as opportunities to initiate a conversation with a customer that could lead to a future opportunity. People do not want more information; they want insight. This is information beyond the obvious, and they want the clarified information in the context of advice on what to do.

Some sales stories become legends, and here is one I often think about. A sales team comprised of a director and two account managers was holding a quarterly business review at a customer's manufacturing site. This team managed a number of sales interactions with different people in the company. While the meeting was going on, Becky, one of the account managers, left to meet a stakeholder who was not attending the QBR. While she was gone, the discussion turned to outcomes and metrics. The question came up about the number of widgets produced in a day on the line. No one knew the answer. Quite boldly, the sales director said, "Don't worry. When Becky gets back, she will know the answer." Sure enough, a little while later, Becky returns to the conference room and realizes all eyes are on her. She asks, "What?" and they turn to her and ask how many widgets come off the line every day. She said, "That's easy. 11,500." That is a great story because the people in the company didn't even know the answer, but their account manager did. There can be no question that Becky was serving as an advocate for her customer.

The Success Plan

The best way that you can advocate for your customer is to work with them on a specific success plan. Every person, every business, has performance and/or business goals. Sometimes those goals are defined clearly as Key Performance Indicators (KPIs) and other kinds of metrics, but often people either get stuck in the big picture of doubling their revenue or they get stuck in the micro weeds of counting the minutes people spend on the phone. Companies have all kinds of ways that they measure their success, including a Net Promoter Score (NPS), which they use to determine if customers are willing to refer them to others. So often, there are online locations where reviewers can post comments and review their experience. Additionally, companies will have internal metrics that they track. The interesting thing is that so often they'll be tracking some kind of metric, but they don't always connect it back up to the company strategy or goal. For many years in sales, we would often look at that big business goal, such as a plan to double revenue in the next two years. While everyone believed they were contributing to that goal in their own way, it would be hard to find those contributing criteria that we could, in fact, use to influence with our project.

Setting up a success plan discussion with your customer is a really good idea. First and foremost, it is a great conversation to have. You can begin by asking: *What are you measuring already? What do you want to measure?* The interesting thing about this is that so many times salespeople push this conversation off to the end or never have it at all. Then they try to come back after the fact and do some kind of forensic goal setting, which never really works. Making the success plan a part of your effort to advocate for the customer provides you a path to value. And that value is the basis for future sales. Think of it as your promise, and then once the promise is kept, it's very easy to go back and say, "Look what we did for you already. Let's do some more."

How do you create a success plan? For the past fifty years, training organizations have used the Kirkpatrick model for evaluation. There are four phases and they have accomplished the first two very well. You have probably filled out a smile sheet after a class, and that is phase 1—the user experience. You have likely taken a test or quiz, and that is knowledge evaluation or phase 2. Where evaluating has been tricky is in the second half of the model, which is phase 3, behavior change, and phase 4, business results. This model applies quite easily to sales. In the case of a software project, for example, you would want to ensure the people are prepared to do whatever they need to do with the sofware by asking if they have the right information. The real magic occurs when you examine the third stage of behavior change since it is always tied to everything. The most interesting aspect of this is that it is not always discussed or even brought up in conversation. Clearly, if you had management software you were trying to sell, the behavior change that your client is looking for is the reason they're buying this software. Finding out what that behavior change is supposed to be enables you to set a metric for success and then track that change as part of your value to the customer. The fourth stage is, of course, business value. You can map the change in their behavior because they got whatever you sold them; they are able to contribute to their business goal. Here's where it gets interesting. If your software or your tool or your widget or whatever you're selling is everything to everybody, then it can provide 100% of the return on investment and it will do everything you can imagine including double the revenue and make the world a perfect place to live in. In reality, that product is just part of the picture, so it is going to contribute to part of the metric. This is where you estimate it. And this is where you don't exaggerate it or make some kind of hollow claim. You're not a TV commercial; you're an advocate for their business. You must have an honest conversation with them. *We think if you use our software, you will reduce the time it takes for employees to accomplish whatever you do so you will see more completions of this activity. You will see a reduction in errors and fewer instances of expedited shipping because those errors caused delays.* Having that conversation is powerful, and it is an important one to have early on.

METRICS TO MEASURE SUCCESS

Now just like talking about money, people get nervous talking about metrics and objectives. To that I say there is nothing to be nervous about. This is an important conversation to have, and a lot of times your clients and customers will appreciate the opportunity. They may be unclear on exactly what is measured, and this may be the first time they have really thought about it in a proactive way. Often, they will engage with others in your client base and really kind of workshop it with you. As soon as I said that I see you rolling your eyes that this would become a long-term consultancy, but it really isn't. It is simply a matter of asking: *What do you measure already? What would you like to influence in behavior and in your business? What would you like to happen differently?*

You can even apply this to retail sales. Let me tell you a funny story about my husband. Years and years ago, when we were first married, my husband was a commercial appraiser, and he used the HP 12C calculator. This pocket-sized handheld calculator had all kinds of built-in functions that enabled users to perform advanced calculations. It was quite a popular item for people in appraising real estate or mortgage banking. So, when the fancy new HP 19B came out there was quite a bit of buzz in the industry. We were looking at it in a department store in the Boston area and my husband tried to convince me that it was worth buying. He said it was fantastic, and I told him that he already had a fantastic calculator. This one cost well over $135, and it seemed like buying something we already had was a ridiculous waste of money. So, my husband constructed a success plan. He proceeded to explain to me that because the calculator reduced the number of keystrokes with more built-in functions than the other one, he was going to save time. He then proceeded to calculate the number of seconds he was going to save, and therefore he could spend more time with me. At the time, I thought that was a pretty funny argument, and probably I would not very likely perceive those added seconds in my day with him. I did appreciate his success plan and agreed to get the calculator. The truth of the matter is, he was converting the change in behavior associated with using this new device to something that was of value to me in order to make his case. He was building a business case to prove value just like you do every day.

To advocate for your customer, you must put that business case in their context. A bulleted list of "typical" outcomes is a great conversation starter, but as a REAL Seller you need to establish a success plan. You should identify as early as possible what the value to your prospect is. Use what I call a flipped Kirkpatrick model. In 1959, Donald Kirkpatrick built the famous four-level training evaluation model that has stood the test of time. Since then, it has undergone some revision, but fundamentally, it is still the same four levels mentioned earlier—the user reaction to the experience, the increase in required knowledge, the behavioral change needed, and the business results. And those four areas that have been used in training also apply to your success plan today. I look at it as defining what the user needs to know, to do, to say differently based on whatever I am selling them. Now you are probably thinking, *Why would I use a 50-year-old model designed for training in my next sales engagement?* My reply to that is, *Why break what is not broken?* Consider this model to build the success plan as part of your business case. Look at it as an organic process requiring multiple conversations and exploration over time both before and after the sale.

Take a look at the current state by asking "what do you measure now?" and identify metrics that might be influenced by your product or service. Through multiple conversations, negotiate the metric that you intend to achieve and the method to measure it. Don't settle for smile sheets and adoption reports. Think about this in terms of a SaaS sale. You want to sell and install your application at the customer. At the same time, you want that license agreement to last. Establishing metrics for each of the categories in the Kirkpatrick model supports your promise of value. Why is it flipped? Instead of beginning with the traditional level-1 evaluation similar to what you might see in a review posting on Amazon, you must begin with the tough side—level 3, behavior change, and level 4, business results. So, the categories are the same. Well, of course they are. Our focus is just different.

In the flipped Kirkpatrick model, you will explore the behavior change that the company expects to happen and set a metric for influencing business results. In my husband's case it was the fact that he would be able to calculate things in less time. The real business value, for me, was the added moments that I could spend with him.

Think about your success plan as part of the way that you

advocate for your customer. Here's the added benefit that happens by having this conversation with your key stakeholder. You are actually empowering that person to go back inside their company and share that understanding of the value with others above them. By doing that you're elevating them as the hero in the process, and that is how you become a true advocate for the customer.

A Is for Advocate: Thought Generator

Some ideas to noodle on prior to meeting with your prospect or customer:

1. When you think about your customer, what will be different for them once they buy your product?
2. What key criteria for business success can your product influence?
3. What insight can you share with your customer to support their business success?
4. How can you represent the business value of your product or solution to your customer?

Chapter 6

L IS FOR LEAD TO THE SOLUTION

"Persuasion is often more effectual than force."

— Aesop

By now I'm sure you realize that REAL Selling is about being your authentic self. Like every acronym, and therefore every word, every letter is important. But in the case of REAL Selling, the L may matter more than the other letters. L stands for Lead to the Solution. This is the true differentiator for a REAL Seller. It is the true competitive differentiator for a seller in these current times.

Think about when new technology or a totally new innovative product is launched. We often think of it as selling itself. This is happening a great deal in the software-as-a-service (SaaS) industry, where sellers often believe that if they just show their software to someone that person will be so thrilled they'll just sign on the dotted line for a multi-year contract. We experience this ourselves as buyers because we all have multiple streaming services that often overlap in their content. We just seem to sign up sight unseen. Remember, if buyers just want to see a product, they can search online. They don't need a salesperson if the product sells itself. They need a business partner who is a REAL Seller.

The Best Idea Is When You Think of My Idea

The modern buyer relies on a REAL Seller to offer insight and serve as a trusted advisor. By leading to the solution rather than with the solution, you put the customer at the center of every conversation. You establish clarity on the success plan and its focus on business value. This approach is quite different from solution selling. Those were the days where you basically guessed what keeps them up at night and offered some shiny solution right in the early stages. This, of course, led to the price wars and discount demands. By leading to the solution, you take the approach that the best idea is when you think of my idea. Using the REAL methodology, you will have held conversations rather than interviews. With the insights and success planning, you will lead them to the moment when they themselves suggest buying your solution.

In every phase of the sales cycle, you will feel the pull of cosmic selling energy to jump to the solution. You will want to shout out your solution and close the deal. That might work for you once in a while, but in the current environment of knowledgeable buyers it is crucial that you differentiate yourself as a valued partner rather than a transactional seller. As you lead to the solution, recognize your effort along the way to build trust, share insights, and build that long-lasting relationship. It will prove to be the bigger payoff than that quick transaction.

Challenger Taught Us to Dance

The Challenger books introduced us all to the elements of the commercial teaching choreography. The six stages begin with the warmer. The warmer is the opening where you establish trust with the customer while you listen carefully to their situation, show empathy for whatever is going on with them, share with them your understanding of the industry and the pressures that they are under, and how you feel for them. This will help them trust in you and believe what you say. And remember in a high-trust environment people make decisions easier and faster. During the warmer you're actually establishing this collaborative environment which will form a foundation for your future conversations, and if that is established well, then the rest should follow pretty easily.

In the next stage, you must reframe the problem, providing a new perspective on the situation. Generally, this means they are giving you a problem that represents a particular point in time with one particular situation. Because you are looking at it as a challenger you're looking at it strategically, how it fits in the big picture—the global picture of the company. You have to reframe that problem in a way that will actually disrupt or challenge that customer to think beyond that simple request. The reframe is one of the more difficult challenges for you from a skill perspective. Your natural instinct would be to start showing them solutions and other shiny objects that you have delivered to other customers. This is the first big difficulty. Some of the other steps are more difficult from an emotional perspective because you're pushing the customer pretty hard, but in this case you need to really probe, listen, and understand strategically. You need to think about the big picture of the customer. You must know a lot about those market trends, and the general needs that result from them.

At this point, you begin to explore the bad news associated with doing nothing. You're telling them the real magnitude of the problem. And if you want to get really simplistic about it, it's like if you have a toy that requires four batteries and one of those batteries gets corroded. You start thinking how expensive batteries are and maybe it might be a good idea just to buy one battery and replace the one that got corroded since the others seem fine. A transactional seller would sell you the one battery and call it a day. A Challenger seller would talk about what you are trying to do and provide insight into how you're actually putting stress on the system by having one fresh battery and three old batteries. And furthermore, you're not gaining anything because in the long run when the whole thing dies, you're going to buy four new batteries to replace them all. That means that instead of buying four batteries now, you're going to have to buy five batteries in total later. While that's a rather simplistic example, the idea is that you really want to pull them out of themselves for a minute and think about that bigger picture.

Let's talk about phase four of the Challenger choreography, which is the emotional impact. You can see how up to this point you've really been talking about things that aren't exactly emotional. Your conversation has been more practical and tactical up to this point. Now, you want to focus on the emotional impact, which is really the lowest point in the conversation. The reason they call it a Challenger choreography is because you see points where the customer is very positive and very high, and then there are points where the customer is shocked or worried and very low. And you are kind of dancing your way through that up-and-down. So here is where you go from the implications of doing nothing to the actual future state of continuing as is. Often this means explaining rising costs, and that is where it really hits them in the heart or in the wallet. We know that in reality people care about only a couple of things. They don't want to waste money. They don't want to regret their purchases. They don't want to waste time. They have a certain amount of work they need to get done, and if they are unable to do that work, it's a horrible price for them to bear. So often if we can put things in terms of money and time, it will mean something to the customer—and that's what forms the emotional impact. The challenge for you is to make it personal. You must know about their situation or their company or industry and then put everything in their context. It can't just be in a general context for everyone.

The final phase of the conversation is the new way forward, and this is where you kind of pull them out of that emotional impact. *You know it doesn't have to be that bad. We can work together and come up with something that's really going to help you. It's going to be different, but it's going to be better.* You are offering them a framework to address their problem, which in this case is tied to value and differentiators. And that lays the perfect groundwork to present your solution in alignment with the metrics and goals you set in your success plan. Now, they're ready to sign. And that's the intent. The main thing to remember here is that if you follow those six phases and recognize the sort of ups and downs of the customer's emotional experience, it gives you a very solid path to lead to the solution.

There are a few things to remember about this. First, the Challenger choreography doesn't have to happen in a single conversation. It is a framework that could cover multiple customer interactions. It also leads you to the solution, but the success plan carries you further. By establishing your goals and metrics at the front end in your success plan and following the framework to lead to the solution, you are now prepared for that long-term valued partnership where you can go back and discuss the progress against the success plan and expand the sale further in the future.

THE EXPANSION SALE

REAL Sales Methodology is not just a construct for the new customer. It can be very effective with an existing customer. Existing customers know you and they expect you to be their valued partner. For that reason, they are open to having you teach them something new. This gives you an opportunity to talk to them specifically about their business situation and build on the value you've already provided to them to expand the sale going forward. And this is not always a bed of roses because sometimes they are not so happy. But an unhappy customer can be an opportunity as much as a happy customer. Serving as a customer-centric advocate and using your skills in commercial teaching will enable you to leverage their objection as a buying cue that you can turn into an opportunity for a new way forward. This leads to another solution that you will sell them. This way you will lead to the next sale.

Remember, challenging the customer to think about their situation differently, even if it's a situation that you have established with them prior, can be an opportunity for sales. Selling is not a one-time event and your relationship with your customer is ongoing. We refer to this as customer health. Just like a medical doctor evaluates your health, you can evaluate the health of your customer. Are they happy? Are you meeting your goals with them? Are you helping them meet their goals? Have they got any complaints at all? And you can even rank them as sort of red/yellow/green to determine who you want to take a look at. Some of the customers who might be struggling a bit might not have you to blame, but rather they're struggling because they're only doing a small amount of business with you and the rest of their business is being delivered late or not giving them the value that they want. Again, this becomes an opportunity. So, evaluating the customer health is really a foot in the door for conversations that lead to expansion sales.

The Roadmap To A Valued Partnership

Often salespeople will think that once they get to the paperwork, then they are just pushing paper and pressuring timelines, handing the deal off to someone else. Nothing could be further from the truth. You still own their success and should ensure a smooth hand-off to others on the team.

Expanding your footprint in an account might be a personal goal or one someone else has set for you. Continuing the conversation you began in the first deal will help lay the foundation for success even if you are beginning with a new stakeholder contact. When you consider the emotional drivers for buying, they are often grounded in safety or risk aversion. And while these appear to be emotional reasons from the heart, the customers themselves may consider them logical reasons from the head. This means representing your success plan and current state of progress would appeal to both. The critical success factor here is you, the salesperson. The knowledge and capability that you bring to the table is a differentiator for the solution. Often, by being a valued and knowledgeable partner, you make the difference in the sale because you can appeal on both the emotional and logical plane. Don't discount the power of the personal touch. The most common reasons to buy are time, money, energy, and convenience. These are all very specific values to the customer, both new and existing. You can ensure that it is easy to buy from you and that you will be checking in on them because you care about their success, and that you are always available to them.

L IS FOR LEAD TO THE SOLUTION: THOUGHT GENERATOR

Some ideas to noodle on prior to meeting with your prospect or customer:

1. Have you established a promise of value to your customer?
2. Have you established a path to a future sale?
3. Have you thought of others in the customer company who might benefit from a conversation with you?
4. Have you truly begun with the end in mind? Was your result more than you expected when you began the engagement?

Chapter 7

Your Next Steps

"A sale is not something you pursue; it's what happens to you while you are immersed in serving your customer."

— Unknown

We've come a long way together in this book, navigating through the letters of the acronym REAL: Research, Engage, Advocate, and Lead to the Solution. There's a lot to think about in preparing and executing a fruitful customer relationship, and I think it's important to just review some key tips and hints that were discussed earlier in this book.

Hints and Tips

Remember that every interaction with your customer is a conversation, not an interview. I can remember having conversations with vendors and account managers from different companies who would ask me question after question without any return to me. Often, I felt like they just had a checklist they had to complete before they could get off the call. I got to the point where I would tell them that they could only ask me three questions, and then they were going to have to tell me something to provide some reason for remaining on the call with them. Had they been a little more personal, a little more empathetic, I would have been much more open to answering their questions. So, the best advice I've ever heard around this subject is to think of it as a conversation with a human and not as some information-gathering discovery process or some other clinical experience that you can imagine. This is REAL Sales Methodology and, while the letters of the words signify the methodology, the word itself means to be authentic. Just be real.

Talk to them as people. The REAL methodology is grounded in the notion of establishing a high-trust environment and employing empathetic listening. You bring a lot to the table in terms of capability and character, and those two criteria form the foundation of the high-trust environment. Demonstrating that as you talk to prospects and customers can only enhance that long-term relationship with your client. It is most important these days that you build a relationship that can last over time. Remember, they can still buy anything online without ever speaking to another person, so you need to make it worth their while to talk to you.

Take the time to listen. There's an old saying that you were given two ears and one mouth for a reason. Listen twice as much as you talk. The more they talk the more you learn about their situation, their needs, and potentially their desire to buy from you. Listening is so critically important, and the best listeners win.

The most important tip of all is one that we focused on in

Chapter 6: Leading to the Solution. The best idea is when you think of my idea. When the customer thinks of the solution themselves and asks you if they can buy, then you're in for the long haul. And that's where you want to be. You want the conversation to go so smoothly and intimately that the client trusts you enough to say *I think we should work on a proposal together* or *I think I'm ready to buy.*

REAL REMINDERS

Let's look at some key tips for fulfilling the need to research. The most important thing to remember is that doing your homework does pay off, ensuring that you have the right information. You must understand your customer, their role, the market, their pressures, and the trends that are influencing their decisions right now. There may even be regionally-specific trends and pressures. The business customer is proud of his brand and attached to the company strategy. By having, at least, a fundamental understanding of that prior to meeting with them will matter to your client. It will clearly establish the kind of foundation you want for conversations going forward.

And don't forget your research never ends. Even as you close the call you may walk away with the desire to learn more about their situation. Keep your radar up and you'll find yourself catching news about that sort of thing. So, consider research your ongoing work.

In the engage phase we explored the notion of building a high-trust environment. This is critically important in every relationship, whether personal or business. Trust may feel like a complicated thing. In many ways it is, but if you break it down into its parts, it can be manageable. Be conscious of intent. Remember intent goes both ways. While understanding the intent of your prospect or client is crucial, establishing your own intent is the most important. If your intent is to support the success of your customer, then that permeates every conversation you have with them. They will perceive that you are their valued partner, and that will move your sales process along more quickly.

As part of the engage phase you often must handle objections, and, as I stated earlier in the book, it has often been said that you don't even start to sell until they say no. If trust has been established and your intent is made manifest, then objections and answering their questions and pushback, while not easy, is achievable. Remember to base your answers on the value to them. Relate the insight in the form of a memorable story. Insight stories can make all the difference.

I can remember a story I was told by my manager Ray. For many years he represented a large technology company targeting the banking industry. At the time the technology was new and somewhat untested in the market. His challenge was to foster trust and communicate value to his prospect. He took research seriously and regularly read annual reports and 10Ks in preparation for meeting with a prospect. On one of his research trips he toured his company's manufacturing facilities. He and his guide were watching the production line as the product was coming through. He could see a woman who was examining each product and then putting a sticker on it. Ray asked his guide what she was doing. He said, "Oh that's Marge. Marge is our inspector. Nothing leaves this plant without Marge's sticker on it." That was a powerful image for Ray. Suddenly he realized that he could tell the story of Marge's inspection sticker when his prospects pushed back on how he could prove the quality of the products. That insight story enabled Ray to explain the promise of value to a customer.

Finally, here is a brief reminder to carefully plan those client meetings. It's more than simply sending an online invite or shooting them a thank-you note. Including an agenda is important, but documenting the results of your meeting in what is a modified letter of understanding can really matter a lot in your process. It is a way to track what was discussed, what the action items are, and who is responsible for those actions. It also gives you a sort of digital paper trail, documenting your conversations. It can be a helpful tool to use.

Another important reminder is to include the PAO in every e-mail. PAO stands for Purpose, Agenda, and Outcomes. One of the best examples of the use of a PAO that I have ever heard concerns an account manager at a Software-as-a-Service company. This salesperson prepared to meet a prospect for his manufacturing software by constructing a PAO which he sent in an e-mail prior to the meeting. The CEO of the prospect company responded to that e-mail with a specific list of what he wanted to see during the meeting. He also called out what kind of outcome he was looking for. That kind of information is gold. The account manager adjusted his planned presentation and discussion points to align with the client, and he was able to close the deal. Imagine how long it might have taken him to understand those needs in a traditional discovery conversation. Constructing your PAO is an excellent exercise, and it enables you to clarify what your plan is for that meeting. The idea of sending it ahead of time to the prospect or client just further multiplies the return on your time investment.

Beginning with the end in mind and ensuring you have a solid success plan is something that must occur in every deal. So often companies have not thoroughly explored their own understanding of success metrics. By raising this conversation and helping guide them to at least some rudimentary outcomes is a benefit to them. Remember, it is not just whether they like your product but what is your product going to do for them in terms of supporting the intended behavior of their people and their business results. The key thing to remember is that your starting point is where they are focused now. Ask them what they are already measuring. If they say they do not measure anything, then suggest something. Obviously, many of the products that we sell today automate some functions or help support workers safely, and counting the number of errors and looking for a reduction in that number could be a success metric. One very common and important metric could be time to proficiency, for example, or how much time they save using your product. When you make suggestions, even if they are not correct, you will trigger the answer in your client's mind, and it will make for a very fruitful conversation.

The notion of leading to the solution rather than with the solution is the biggest sea change in sales methodology since sales training began a hundred years ago. Challenger sales promoted this position, and it was truly a game changer. When you lead to the solution you listen more, align to the business more, and uncover more opportunities for sales than if you lead with the solution, expecting your demo of the shiny thing to sell itself. Mahan Khalsa, in his book *Let's Get Real or Let's Not Play*, cautions salespeople to not guess. Guessing is the easiest thing a salesperson can do. In solution selling and in relationship selling, quite frankly, the salesperson is encouraged to guess the solution and lead with that. But just like the negotiator who guessed that cutting the orange in half would solve the problem of the two girls arguing over the orange, people often guess wrong. In the case of the negotiator, he was incredibly happy with himself, but the girls started to cry. One girl wanted to bake a cake with the zest of the orange and the other girl wanted to extract its juice. Because the orange was cut in half, neither could accomplish their goal.

SaaS sellers have the biggest problem right now because their software is the new cool-looking technology. It can feel like if the prospect just sees it, they'll want to buy it. Sellers will guess what prospects want and skip the conversation. They either lose the sale or undersell their product. The reminder is to lead prospects to the solution rather than leading with it.

A further piece of advice around this concerns demos and case studies. Demos and case studies should support the conversation that you're having rather than serve as a separate TV show in the middle of your presentation. Prospects who are asking to see demos are asking to fill a gap in their understanding of how to solve their own problem. This puts the burden of context on you to include the demos and case studies in your story, ensuring that you emphasize the problem that was solved, the value that was perceived, the goals that were intended, and the outcomes that were achieved. Mahan Khalsa says, "Consultants, being the intelligent people we are, formalize the guessing process; we call it a proposal." So, the big reminder here is don't guess.

Don't Stop Learning

Before I close this book, I think it's important to provide some advice on what should be on your bookshelf or in your book bag. There are thousands of books about selling and selling methodologies out there right now. There are likely a million recordings, e-learning resources, and videos of people offering sales advice worth listening to. Currently, I have a brief list of books that I think are worth at least scanning if not studying thoroughly, and I will give you the list in order of my priority for them.

Jeffrey Gitomer's Sales Manifesto by Jeffrey Gitomer

This book is an easy read with, as he says, "imperative actions you need to take and master to dominate your competition and win for yourself for the next decade." This book is one you should just carry around with you, especially when traveling, because it's loaded with tips and stories about ways to be successful. I think of it as a battery charger. One of the key areas of focus is his answer to the question *How can I get better at closing?* Gitomer claims it's not how you close, it's how you open. He offers golden advice about how to handle those important customer conversations. His book was published in 2019 and is perfect for the current challenges salespeople face. He also hosts a daily podcast and offers many resources on his website. Jeffrey Gitomer is one to know.

Let's Get Real or Let's Not Play by Mahan Khalsa & Randy Illig

Even though this book was originally published in 1999, I would still consider this a must-have for any seller today. Khalsa is nothing short of a genius in terms of establishing a framework for successful selling. From his five key beliefs to his advice on structuring a conversation, his teachings are critically important to selling today. He is one of the original founders of the Sales Performance Group of Franklin-Covey and has a considerable library of video resources on his YouTube channel.

The Speed of Trust by Stephen M.R. Covey

Covey says, "Trust is the new currency of our interdependent, collaborative world." His book represented a significant change in thinking for me back in 2006 when I heard him speak at a learning conference. So many times, I had struggled with whatever the force was that slowed down a process. To realize it was all about trust just opened my eyes. This book provides a solid background in the power of trust and the importance of building a high-trust environment for a sales conversation. His bottom line is that the level of trust has consequence, and most importantly, earning trust is a skill that you can study, learn, and cultivate.

The Challenger Sale by Brent Adamson & Matthew Dixon

It is hard to imagine anyone who has not been exposed in some fashion to Challenger selling. This research- and data-based methodology for sales has been a dramatic disruptor in the world of selling. It's focused on the buying process and the buyer's journey. It also defines personas of both the sellers and the stakeholders in an account. As someone in sales training and enablement, I often hear that a salesperson either totally bought into the Challenger methodology, or they just can't stand it. My sense is that in some ways it is more complex than they think. They then try some elements and feel like it just doesn't work for them. The truth is, the key concepts of the Challenger methodology support that important long-term relationship after you have established yourself as a valued partner. My recommendation is that it is here to stay, and everyone should read it and absorb its message because, even if we've moved on, the future is built on the Challenger methodology.

Insight Selling by Michael Harris

If you Google insight selling, you will see that this generic term for a sales approach has been addressed by many authors.

The book I have selected here for your book bag is *Insight Selling* by Michael Harris. This 100-page paperback gives you a lot of guidance on how to construct insight stories to prove value to your customers. It's concise and easy to follow. I like it because it offers some very practical and actionable techniques for creating industry insight stories, which I believe is a critically essential element to any sales conversation.

Everyone Sells! How Top Producers Make Top Dollars by Lee Dubois

In writing a sales training course recently, I was searching around for some resources on handling objections, and I came upon a summary of a framework by Lee Dubois from his book. He has a quite easy-to-follow method for handling objections. I am calling him out here because he has some online videos and other coaching tools available that might help in this area. This book is out of print but available used.

In Closing

When I taught high school, I knew what my purpose was. My intention was to enable the growth and success of young people as they prepare to graduate high school and start their own lives. But on the first day I sat in my cubicle in a corporate setting as a sales-training instructional designer, I was baffled as to why I was there. I thought maybe I was there just to make money for "the man." And I knew that would not be good enough for me. But then I realized that I was there to enable the success of others. As my career evolved, I soon realized my intent was to enable the success of salespeople like you. The intent to enable the success of salespeople has ruled my life since then and has been the thread through every project I have completed and every award that I've ever achieved. My intention continues with this book, in hopes that it helps you succeed as well. Please let me know if it does.

Acknowledgements

People have asked me how I could write this book so quickly, and my answer is always the same. I have been thinking it through since 1998 when I wrote my first sales training course. All the salespeople, trainers, sales enablement professionals, and sales gurus I have met over the years left an impression on me. Add that to the old Vermont common sense I was born with, and the REAL Sales Methodology sprang fully grown from my head.

There are two brilliant people who are no longer walking the earth, taken too soon, who left an indelible impression on me. Jon Raphaelson was a business consulting genius, and I was privileged to work with him. His insight was like a bright light in a dark tunnel. Dru Matthews was a creative and talented sales training mastermind. We would stride the world like titans building award-winning training together. I miss them both every day and I often ask myself: *What would Jon say? What would Dru do?*

Additionally, I must acknowledge two of my "Girl Team 2000" colleagues who worked closely with me over the years and helped me navigate the wonderful world of sales training: Becky Tise and Judy Blachek. Becky was a REAL Seller before the methodology was even defined. She went on to be an extraordinary sales trainer and coach. She was the instructor for my first sales training course—the 509—selling AlphaServers for Digital Equipment Corporation! Judy taught me everything I have come to know about functioning in the corporate world. She is still one of the best sales training writers I know, although she never wants to admit it.

The inspiration for putting words to the page came directly from my colleagues at Infopro Learning. Anu Galhotra worked on one of my project teams when she was first starting out in the industry, and we reconnected in the past few years. She is Senior Vice President of Strategy and Solutions at Infopro and very generously invited me to serve on her team as a Learning Strategist and the Lead for the Sales Training Practice. One day she asked me when I was writing my book. In parallel I began working with Dan Rust. He also found his way to Infopro after many years in leadership training and coaching. He is the genius behind the REAL acronym, which he used in early iterations of his training program. He very kindly and generously gifted the acronym to me. The two of them formed the match and the spark to light my fire. Also thank you to Preetam Shetty, Enterprise Sales Rep at Infopro, for his kind yet honest feedback.

There are so many others who have added to that sales cauldron I call a brain. Thank you all!

Finally, I cannot complete this without acknowledging my beloved family. Since I have worked from a home office for over 20 years, my husband Bill and children Ariel and Solomon have had to work around me every day. To their probable chagrin I never worked in a closed-off room but always in the middle of the action. I accomplish nothing in this world without the love and support of my family. Thank you.

For further study of the REAL Sales Methodology or other training requirements, please contact infoprolearning.com and tell them Carol Cohen sent you!

www.ingramcontent.com/pod-product-compliance
Lightning Source LLC
Chambersburg PA
CBHW031446210526
45464CB00005B/2349